WASTE of TIMELESSNESS

and other early stories

by

Anaïs Nin

This book is a special edition
published by Magic Circle Press
Weston, Connecticut

and

Distributed by Walker & Company
720 Fifth Avenue
New York, New York, 10019

Library of Congress catalog number: 74-28648
ISBN: 0-8027-0569-3

Grateful acknowledgment is hereby made to the Library of North-
western University for access to its collection of literature by Anaïs
Nin.

Fabric art: Sas Colby
Design coordination: Johanna Shields
Photo by: Margo Moore

Printed in the United States of America

PREFACE

    I had never intended these stories to be published, knowing they were immature. But then I realized that it is valuable for other writers to follow the development of the total work, to observe each step of the maturing process. From the point of view of today's achievements, we tend to judge our first work harshly. When young writers tend to become discouraged comparing their work with a mature work, it is good for them to look back at what was being written at their age so they can measure the distance between the beginning and the final synthesis.

    Two elements appear here which were to be affirmed in later work: Irony and the first hints of feminism.

    I was persuaded by Valerie Harms that these stories would be for those who understand and love my work and are interested in the progression. This is a book for friends only.

ANAIS NIN

WASTE OF TIMELESSNESS

I t was the usual invitation to a usual houseparty, the usual people, and with her usual husband. Why must it be friends of the "great writer" Alain Roussel rather than Alain Roussel himself who invited them out for the weekend?

Besides, it was raining.

The first thing Mrs. Farinole said was: "It has not rained here all summer. What a pity it should today, of all days! It will be impossible for you to imagine how perfectly lovely this place can be."

"Oh, but I can very easily imagine," she answered and looked around appreciatively at the hills, the pines, the sea quite formally framed to make a cozy windless nook. And then she imagined a gigantic gust of wind sweeping the whole place clean, and Mrs. Farinole saying: "I am so sorry, our house has flown away, and so I cannot ask you to spend the night. I shall have to telephone the carpenter. He must do something about it immediately."

And then Alain Roussel would happen to pass by in quest of material, carrying a crab net. Seeing her on the road he would say: "Will you come with me? We can spend the weekend on that old fishing boat on the beach. It is a grand place." (He would use another word, a better one than "grand" but she could not think of it just at that moment.)

Her husband would say: "Wait a minute then. I must get her raincoat. She is subject to neuritis."

"There is Roussel's house," said Mrs. Farinole. "He has painted his gate in turquoise green. It will soon turn grey with the sea air."

"Have you read all his books?" she asked.

"We will, by and by," said Mr. Farinole. "Did you know that he wrote the last three right here?"

"And while they were repairing his house, too," said Mrs. Farinole. "I don't know how he could do it."

"And his cook was ill — the house was terribly disorganized," added Mr. Farinole.

"He wrote something very extraordinary in a magazine," she said.

"He *is* a very extraordinary man," said Mr. Farinole. "Did you ever hear how he repaired his own oar when the mechanic could not make out what was the matter?"

"And here is our house," said Mrs. Farinole. "Henry, show her the stubborn wisteria."

They paused in front of the door.

"Do you see this wisteria? It was a stubborn plant — insisted on growing to the left for two years, and at last I got it around to the right, and over the door, where I wanted it."

During this story little Mrs. Farinole shone with pride. "That is just like Henry, to be so *beautifully* persistent."

"Do you think," she asked, "that he could make me grow to the right too? I would really like to grow to the right, and over the door, but it seems impossible."

Mr. Farinole laughed, "You have Irish in you, have you?"

"No, why?"

"Whenever Henry says something funny we said: "You have Irish in you, have you?"

"You do!"

"And he, invariably answers. 'And a little Scotch besides!'"

"Now," said Mrs. Farinole, "you know the family's pet joke."

"I think that is delicious," she said. For a little while she did not hear the rest of the conversation. She was thinking that she would like to ask Roussel what he meant by intuitional reasoning. "By intuitional reasoning," she thought, "I could be made to grow to the right, and over the door, but not by reasoning alone."

They walked to the end of the garden.

"What is that? A boat? A boat in this garden?"

"I will show you," said Mr. Farinole. "It was here when we got the house. It is an old Norman fishing boat, used as a tool house. See, it is black because they put tar on it to preserve it. What a shape it has eh? So deep, so fat, so comfy, so safe looking."

"May I look inside, oh, may I?"

"We put a bed there once for a little boy guest. He insisted on sleeping there. He got such a thrill out of it!"

The inside smelt of tar. There was a bed, several old trunks, garden tools, pots, seeds, and bulbs. There was a tiny square window on each side of the door. The roof sloped down squatly.

"Oh, I would like to sleep here too." she said.

"Have you Irish in you?" said Mrs. Farinole.

"Think of your neuritis," said her husband.

"Henry is awfully proud of that boat," said Mrs. Farinole.

"I hear the dinner bell," he said evasively and modestly.

It was all so much easier since she knew about the existence of the boat — so much easier to jump gaily from topic to topic, being always careful not to exceed a certain moderate temperature.

There was the boat waiting in the dark garden, at the end of the very narrow path, the boat with its little twisted doorway, its small windows, the peaked roof, its smell of pungent tar . . . the very old boat which had travelled far, now sunk in a quiet dark garden.

The atmosphere in the Farinoles' library was dense with laughter. She must not stop laughing. Her husband had said: "The Farinoles have the most delightful sense of humor." There was nothing to be done about it.

It was bedtime.

The Farinoles did not believe that she meant to sleep on the boat, not until she was half way down the path, with her nightgown under her arm. Then they shouted: "Wait! Wait! We'll walk down with you."

"I know the way," she called back, running faster.

"You will need a candle."

"Never mind, there is a sickly moon, it will do."

Then they called out something else but she did not hear them.

She walked around the boat. It was tied to an old tree. She unfastened the mildewed rope. "And now I am gone," she said, stepping into the boat and banging the little door after her.

She leaned out of one of the windows.

The sickly moon was covered by a cloud.

The wind rushed once through the garden.

She sat on her bed and cried: "I would really like to go away. I would like never to see the Farinoles again. I would like to be able to think aloud, not always in hushed secrecy." She heard the sound of water. "There must be a trip one can take and come back from changed forever. There must be many ways of beginning life anew if one has made a bad beginning. No, I do not want to begin again. I want to stay away from all I have seen so far. I know that it is no good, that I am no good, that there is a gigantic error somewhere. I am tired of struggling to find a philosophy which will fit me and my world. I want to find a world which fits me and my philosophy. Certainly on this boat I could drift away from this world down some strange wise river into strange wise places . . ."

In the morning the boat was no longer in the garden.

Her husband took the 2:25 train home to talk this problem over with his partner.

The boat was drifting down a dark river.

There was no end to the river.

Along the shores there were plenty of landing places, but they were very ordinary looking places.

Roussel had a house on the banks. When she made as if to pay him a visit he asked: "Do you admire me?"

"I love your work," she said.

"And no one else's?"

"I do care for Curran's poetry, and Josiam's criticisms."

"Don't stop here," said Roussel. And she saw that he was surrounded with ecstatic worshippers, so she pushed her boat away.

Along the shore she saw her husband one day. He signalled to her: "When are you coming home?"

"What are you doing this evening?" she asked.

"Having dinner with the Parks'."

"That is not a destination," said she.

"What *are* you headed for?" he shouted.

"Something big," she answered, drifting away.

More quiet shores unfolded. There was nothing resplendent or marvellous to see. Little houses everywhere. Sometimes little boats tied to a stake. People used them for small rides.

"Where are you going?" she asked them.

"Just resting from ordinary living," they said, "off for a few hours for just a little fantasy."

"But where are you going?"

"Back home after a while."

"Is there nothing better further on?"

"You're stubborn," they said coldly. She drifted away.

The river had misty days and sunny days, like any other river. Occasionally there was magic; moments of odd stillness when she felt the same intense exaltation she had experienced the first night on the boat, as if she were at last sailing into unutterable living.

She looked out of the little window. The boat was sailing very slowly and going nowhere. She was beginning to get impatient.

On the shores she saw all her friends. They called out to her cheerfully but formally. She could feel that they were hurt. "And no wonder," she thought, "they must have sent me many invitations and I have not answered them."

Then she passed Roussel's place again. Now she was sure she had travelled in a circle. He called out to her: "When are you coming home? The Farinoles need their garden tools, and the trunks, too."

"I would like to know," she called out, "what you mean by intuitional reasoning?"

"You can't understand," he called back. "You have run away from life."

"It was the boat which sailed away." she said.

"Don't be a sophist," he said. "It sailed away at your own bidding."

"Do you think that if I came ashore we could have a real talk? I feel then that I might not be wanting to travel."

"Oh," said Roussel, "but it might be *me* who would want to travel. I do not like perfect intimacy; you might write an article about it."

"You're missing something," she said. "It would be an interesting article." And she drifted away.

The shores still offered commonplace scenery, and there was no world beyond.

Her husband called out to her: "When are you coming home?"

"I wish I were home now," she said.

The boat was in the garden. She tied up the cord to the old tree.

"I hope that you had a good night," said Mrs. Farinole. "Come and see our wisteria. It has grown to the left after all, in spite of everything."

"During the night?" she asked.

"Have you Irish in you? Don't you remember how the wisteria looked twenty years ago when you first came to our house?"

"I have been wasting a lot of time," she said.

THE SONG IN THE GARDEN

She discovered that there was something unusual about herself when she refused to pamper her dolls like babies, to air them in baby carriages, to dress them in diapers, and to talk down to them. She consecrated them men and women whose actions scandalized her family when they realized the dolls were an unconscious parody of them. But later, she made no more pretense of handling their lifeless and expressionless bodies, and played with other things.

There was at first hand herself. She found this a rather varied spectacle. Staring at others, asking personal questions was useless. She did not get any answers, or the answers were postponed to a distant date when she could understand, and the staring brought her nothing but exile from the rooms where things really happened.

So she watched herself as if she were an insect. She discovered first of all that she cried when her mother sang. It was a very delectable sensation, which moved the whole inside of her body, swelled, and overflowed, and then died down slowly to a sweet peace. It was a wonderful feeling. The taste of tears was unlike anything she had ever tasted.

She then tried to find out if this happened to other girls of her age. She had a classmate who had a sullen face, and questioned her. No, said the classmate, she had never heard of anything more foolish. One cried if beaten by a teacher, if one bruised one's knee, if one were deprived of the four-o'clock bread and chocolate by irate parents. Or if some rough brother smashed one's favorite doll's face under his electric train, as hers had done, to find out if his train could really run over people.

"Or perhaps," said the classmate, "your mother has a frightening voice. My daddy has one like that."

This drove her to making a more general investigation. Then she learned that the feeling was by no means universal, and that what Dora felt when she had an earache, and Matilda when her savings box was stolen, was altogether different. As for the taste of tears it could not compete with chocolate.

She was gripped by a joy which filled her to overflowing, and which almost eclipsed the feeling of sadness, at the discovery that she was the only person in the world to be visited by such peculiar moods. This joy too, she was to find out, did not exist in her classmates.

So she sat longer in the corner of the balcony, in a small wicker chair, between two flower pots, and two cages filled with tropical birds, and cuddled herself in her own arms as she had never cuddled a rag doll, because so many odd things moved inside of her which were superior to the deadness of dolls.

As soon as it grew dark and cool, her mother and father went out for slow walks, to forget the heat of the day, and the wild glare of the sun. Ramona, the Valencian maid, would put her to bed and entrust her to all the Saints in heaven, and instead of staying to watch her until she fell asleep, she went out to the plaza, by the fountain, where a sailor awaited her. The Saints, however, did not grant sleep to those who were stirred by queer feelings, as if they carried tickling, feathery insects in their chests.

She lay awake, and in the dark she felt something in herself stirring and fluttering. It occurred to her that she might be growing wings, such as she had seen in holy books. The nuns had called wings a soul. She must have that, certainly. It must be that which bothered her when her mother sang. And it was that which grew in the night when Ramona was not there to watch.

But her mother and father, not knowing about it, attributed it all to the heat, and the fever which was spreading in the city, and they sent her to the beach.

She found the beach even more interesting than the balcony. She was quite free to discover it. Ramona's sister with whom she

was staying, was always busy with the housework and mending her husband's fishing nets. The white plaster house they lived in was on the very edge of the beach, and its green shutters could be seen from all the sand dunes and cliffs, so that she could never get lost.

Maria had a daughter, Lola, who was also twelve, and who had a habit of laughing at everything. It seemed to her that Lola knew even less than the other girls in the city. When you make such a lot of noise, run, laugh, scream, jump, sing, call out to everybody, wave to the fishing boats, you can't possibly hear what goes on inside of you. She found in herself an echo of the sounds of the sea, just as if she were a hollow shell, and the colors and smells affected her differently than the singing. They did not bring peace, but an urge to run against the wind, to swim far, and to breathe deeply. But instead of laughing endlessly, of calling out to fishing boats, and of talking continuously at the dinner table, she wrote verses behind her holy pictures.

"Are they hymns?" asked Lola, reading them laboriously. They were about the sea, as if the sea were alive and singing, and hissing like a monster; about the wind, as if the wind had a human voice; about the sand through which she had looked while pouring it over and over against the sunlight, and which she thought powdered jewels; about the crabs she had watched in the hollows of the cliffs; about the foam which she fancied made with soap.

"I thought," said Lola, "that one only wrote hymns to God and the Virgin."

"That has been done," she answered. "But I like to write about things I have seen for myself."

She saw him first. He was a tramp, but not quite like the others who passed almost every day. He wore a hat, long hair, and though he was without a shirt, he was neither blind, nor legless, and his face was clean.

"Oh, Senora," he begged of Maria, "give me a piece of soft coal; you'll see what a beautiful picture I can draw on your wall."

"You will get it dirty," said Maria.

"It rubs off easily. I'll clean it myself. Oh, give me a piece of soft coal, a rather long and thin one if possible. I'll draw you and the Senoritas."

He drew them as they stood there, Lola fat and laughing with embarrassment, her eyes hidden by humorous wrinkles; Maria with a quiet resigned face under the handkerchief she tied under her chin; she with eyes like two question marks; and even the door half open behind them, the bench, a corner of the fishing net hanging from the low roof, the bunch of garlic, and a quilt hanging out of the window.

When he was finished Maria gave him bread and fish.

"Shall I rub it off?" asked the tramp.

"No, no. We will show it to Paco when he comes home."

But Paco stayed two days at sea, and when he came home the drawing was partly effaced, so he merely grunted at it.

But she had found a way to illustrate the hymns so that even Lola could not fail to grasp their meaning.

At first she had wanted to be a Saint because they wore such lovely gowns and gold halos around their hair; afterwards a beggar who would travel wide, drawing people with soft coal. But now it was irrevocably decided that the only thing that counted was what Lola called hymns. In that way she could not only invoke caressingly all the things she loved, the sea, the trees, the sand, the wind, the sun, but she could own them, gather them up to herself, and by reading the hymns over and over again renew each time the feeling she saw at the same time as the object themselves.

This became clearer to her still when she was taken back to the city, and left again on the balcony. She wished for herself those careless days on the beach, and was able to have them. But the secret of those hymns weighed on her mind, and she thought it was time to confess. She showed them to her mother. And her mother began to cry. What a queer thing? What was there in singing and hymns that made people cry. Even a full grown soul, as her mother's must be, could cry. And there was no explanation. All her mother would say, when questioned, was that those things were not called hymns.

She was taken into her father's vast library for the first time. He interrupted his work to give her a slender book.

What she found in it was much better than her own.

She felt in that library not at all as if she had come into a roomful of people and they had answered all her questions, and she had been able to stare at them indefinitely, but as if she had suddenly found a door opening into a vaster world where people resembled only vaguely those she had seen at her parent's receptions. In the books they were much more active, more colorful, more interesting. The real General who called on Thursdays, who had a sonorous voice, white gloves and medals, was fatter and slower than those in the stories, and fonder of little cakes than of battles. The ladies she had seen were perfumed, but some of them had too few eyelashes, or hair on their chin, or rasping voices when they sang, or looked at her through lorgnettes which made their eyes look like those of the crabs. And then nothing magnificent ever happened to them.

But in the library she discovered the existence of enormous lands not only covered with thousands of other cities, but castles, forests, haciendas, other beaches, and all of them abounding in incidents and movements. There was treachery, devotion, miracles, strife, death, ferocious jealousy. The ladies did not sit and listen to music only, but rode on horseback, turned into nuns over night, handled guns when necessary, were stolen, or ran away, put poison in glasses of wine, dressed fantastically and far better than the Saints, danced, fanned themselves, made sharp and humourous remarks, wrote secret letters, played tricks on their husbands.

It was all a bit mixed up and not always easy to understand, but at least there were no blank moments as there were at home, no moments of stillness, no days spoiled by bleak teachers, and not much time wasted on prayers.

Far more startling than all this was a certain book she picked out for herself one day when her father was out, having finished the one he had given her. He had warned her not to touch anything but what he chose for her because it would bore her. But as this book stood next to the one she had just read she fancied it would be interesting.

It was. A man gave his friends a big dinner, with candlelight and ample wines; truffles cooked in sand; cakes brought aflame to the table; pheasants with their feathers on, as if ready to fly off, and continuous music. Among the guests was a lady he overwhelmed with compliments. She had, said the book, a pink satin dress which showed as was the fashion, her very rounded shoulders and the beginning of small but very firm breasts. She laughed at all he said, but leaned backwards whenever he leaned over too much. After dinner, and after dancing a little, she found she could not stay up as long as the other guests because she felt dizzy. In her room she did not have the strength to undress, but fell on her bed in a dead sleep. Hours later when all the household was asleep, the host crept into the room. She heard and felt nothing. He undressed her very slowly and lingeringly, caressing each part of her, and kissing her until she lay quite uncovered, and his enjoyment, said the book, made him tremble and wail.

There was a line and a space, and the story took up again with the woman's utter ruin, her desperation at not knowing who was the father of her child, and having lost the love of the man who had wanted to marry her before the fatal party at which she was drugged.

And she who was reading this tried in vain to build up the facts evaded by the space in the book. It was all a mystery. She was stirred by the description of entirely new sensations. It was no longer the wind, the soft nights, the silky brushing of the palm trees, but this man so strangely moved by the woman.

If that had happened to me, she thought, I would not have let myself go to sleep.

For a time all center of sensation seemed to concentrate in her head. There was in it the sharp image of the man and woman, and the image of more colorful but less subtle adventures; and then accumulated ideas of her own, not so easily written now that she was learning new words. The new words penetrated her with a sweetness, sometimes like a caress, and sometimes they burst on her like explosive revelations, filled her with a clamor of joy and excitement. They were miraculous; they not only named what was there before her, but revealed the incredible existence of vaster and even more fantastic worlds, of millions of people outside of those she knew, of lands entirely different from hers, of millions of feelings far more upsetting than those which had overwhelmed her at the sound of music. Faces which had before seemed different only by feature, color, or shape, now assumed numerous and incredible variety. All things which had one face before, like her parents, or at the most two, gladness and sadness, were now animated, changing, haunting, by her own knowledge of what they hid.

Words were not only the light, but eyes themselves, and as they accumulated on those printed pages, accumulated in her mind, they appeared to her, by their potent, hypnotic power undeniably more wonderful than the static bearded God who never spoke, but let strange men speak for Him, sometimes quite badly.

She learned too, that there were words which had been spoiled, which could not be used anymore. Her father growled at her use of the word "soul." "There were words like that," he said, "that had been badly used; they had lost their meaning."

"But what do you do, then, if the thing exists, and you need the word?"

"You never talk about it," he said. "Or you make up another."

But apart from taste in words, she was surprised to find that her parents were impervious to them. Her father who owned six thousand books ate them as placidly as his meals, digested them without excitement, marked their pages with studiousness, and laid them away without any change of expression — or of life. Her mother read less of them, but with docility and quiet respect. Did they really understand what they meant? And if they did, how could they continue to fill their house with uninteresting people, move only between the beach and city, when there was a vast, immense, fantastic world left to explore? Worse still, when she discovered that they had explored those regions, that they had been in India, in Egypt, in Japan, in France, in North America, in Russia, and that it had left no deep dark trace on their faces, and that the stories they told were pleasant, but like geographical descriptions learned at school.

There was no doubt in her head now, that she would have to see and do all that for herself. Her parents may be wise, but in some ways they reminded her of those classmates who preferred chocolate, which was ordinary, and who also preferred to resemble each other.

Five years. Body almost motionless, bound by walls by quiet habits. Her mind swayed and stirred, by a keen restlessness, impatient to live. Yet it clung to the books, as if they would serve her as a key to the whole world. She really believed that the more she read of them the clearer real living would be to her.

She had at last a taste of travelling. Her parents began carefully the pilgrimage of their own youth. They carried guide books, maps, and went to sleep in the trains.

She tried to find in the static face of the physical world the reflection of the meaning she had found in the written words. To find in ruins, in museums, the proofs of written words, the trace of events. She was surprised to find another meaning to it all, her own meaning. The books were not to serve as keys; they were to stand apart, or at best serve as indications. The best they had done was to train her to see, to think her own thoughts. But as far as standing with them on a secure platform, that was an error. She stood alone. She found streets which were not historical, and which were eloquent. She found eyes of people more eloquent than history. Her parents did not think her respectful enough — of other's knowledge. But they had no respect for her own visions. She saw that again things did not affect her as they did others. If the world had been transformed in passing through the minds of writers, it was now also altering as it passed hers. She needed not the key to the universe; the universe was in her.

Fragments packed into the trunks with everything else. Drifting selves one cannot sail away from.

She was remembering a garden. All the children were playing in it. She was pushed and pulled by all of them as they chased a ball which bounced wildly between them. Very unexpectedly there came out of the house and through the garden full of children and sun and noise, a song, a crooning song. She heard it and straightened herself with a start. The song slipped into the garden quietly, and the children went on laughing and shouting. But she had felt an overflow of strange sadness. The song wafted past her and over the hedge, lingeringly. Inside of her it penetrated sweetly and painfully. Something was worth crying for; something in the song.

The playing and shouting stopped; all the little girls gathered around her.

"Did you fall?"

"Did you hurt your knee?"

"What is the matter with you?"

They all bowed their heads over her. The song encircled her, plaintively.

"What is the matter?"

"Do you want a piece of chocolate?"

"Oh, come, don't be a baby."

"Can't you even say what you're crying for?"

The garden was quiet now. The last note of the song hung in the air. The crying died down too, and the little girls skipped away.

"Will you come and play again?"

From inside the house the voice which had sung now called out in a very plain, human tone: "Come in, come in. I've made you some cake!"

In books she could drift independently and indulge her own whims. And this drifting of the body, choiceless, impulsive, unreasoned, was treated with tolerance, and civilized mellowness, a half-sad humor and sense of frailty. Love here was a function, from which the highest pleasure was to be extracted as from an instrument, and only the mechanism was to be admired for its intricacy.

Before she came to the third world, she thought she knew every feeling that could be. But a new dream was revealed to her in this soft and misty language, a language not treacherously musical so that anything trivial spoken in it could sound profound, not irrevocably clear like the second, but poised between the two as if composed of both, and bringing with it a new attitude. If up to now she knew one had to live with fervor, and with intelligence, now she learned one had not only to live for an idea, or die for it, but also fight for it. To passion was added a new quality of profound selection, of resistance to impulse, of deliberate transfiguration. Until now she had seen only something like a configuration, to which one submitted, either through a faintness of the senses, or an indifference to the demands of the mind. It came most sharply to her in the poetry. The poetry, though rich in sensations, in feeling, and in ideas, suggested with words one could put no finger on, the existence of magic, of mystery, of an unseen world.

It seemed to her that the child who could cry, not at a song, but with a premonition of things worth weeping for, led her now into strange worlds, while others, as old as she was now, still preferred chocolates, detective stories, lives labelled and secure like crackers in a jar.

THE FEAR OF NICE

Ⓣhere were two of them, an old man permanently bent with rheumatism over an asthmatic guitar, and a younger man who sang with an operatic aggressiveness. But it was early in the morning, in Nice, and the sunlight dissolved all critical faculties. Besides, Lyndall was overloaded with pennies, there was a spare envelope in the scrap basket, her window was open, and she was doing some disagreeable re-writing. So she leaned over the window and smiled at the serenaders.

How sweet life was! She was swimming in warmth and in light, floating on cotton. Other music was inspiring and ideal, but this was so much more like her own life; out of tune, sometimes, and so often played on cheap instruments, with rheumatic fingers. Hear the funny little note; it reminded her of the time her brand new husband was sea sick on their honeymoon, that screechy one, of the rapacious guides who took the sublime out of their Italian pilgrimage, that long drawn out, wobbly one, of so many other inglorious moments, when her husband corrected the spelling of her exalted paragraphs, when he pronounced some of her most caressing words a "foreign invention not to be mistaken for English as he knew it . . ."

The man leaning over the next window was throwing money in a cigarette box and laughing at the ridiculous melodies, and as Lyndall could see, laughing at her too because she was swaying thoughtfully over the balcony in rhythm with the crooning sounds below.

That evening Lyndall and her husband were having dinner at the Grand Hotel. Lyndall thought there were too many waiters; one to light her cigarette, one to pour the wine, one to present the meat, another the fish, another the dessert, and yet another for the bill.

She tried to find a real meal in that deceptive luxury, but why did her potato salad taste of mint, and her lamb chop look like a flower? The beets were sliced so finely they tasted like air, and the bread vanished with a sound of crisp paper. There was powdered grass on everything, and a permanent wave on the puree of potatoes. A hundred dishes were brought before her on rolling tables but she could not guess what they contained; the vegetables were disguised with pink sauces, the meats were shaped like stars, marbles, scarabs, garnished with candied eyes to look like mice. She gave up guessing, swallowed without tasting, sat with dignity, fed on the anemic music, smoked unreasonably with a show of glistening nails. She had a desire to break her glass in which a stoically faced waiter had just poured water with such an absorbed, conscientious air that she was sure it would taste like champagne.

Then Lyndall noticed that the man who had thrown money at the serenaders sat at a nearby table. He was smiling with his eyes at the food, at the old ladies, at the Dames Seules, at the waiters, at everything, with an equal nonchalance which vaguely annoyed her.

"Oh, but I know that man," said her husband. "He is the Head of the Rubber Stamp Company. I saw him last week on business. I must speak to him."

Introductions. No change whatever in his eyes. He had not seemed to notice Lyndall's unique 1830 face. Even Lyndall's husband resented this. What was the use of having so many painters classify her face as an anachronism in an age of uniform production?

"Not much of a place, this," said Mr. Breman. "It strikes me as a vast expanse of driftwood, for people who got tired doing nothing. It's languid, boneless, oldish . . ."

"From the point of view of a young businessman, yes," said Lyndall's husband.

"Oh, no, personally. Give me real mountains, and a wind that sweeps up the clouds and mental cobwebs."

"I can see you have not been in Europe long enough to succumb to the love of leisure," said Lyndall with a glance which marked the phrase as a compliment. But the Head of the Rubber Stamp Company was impervious.

"Shall we take a walk?"

"I'll lead you," said Lyndall. "I have discovered a wonderful place."

It was a white cement walk, winding down the hill to the sea. It was edged with tropical plants, huge, fierce, bristly cactus, long fingered bushes spreading like octopuses, others flowering like thick leaved cabbages, others writhing like snakes, all of them thick and furry. They grew violently, clinging furiously to the ground, and bringing to mind the desert, jungle, and the bottom of the sea. The sea breeze did not move them. They could never have been young, but must have showed from the first a firm plenitude, and they never grew old, never wrinkled or drooped, but showed to the end a strange agelessness. They were plants without scent or delicacy, growing without earth and mysteriously nourished with sun and water.

The three now shadowy figures bent over them and talked about them. Lyndall was afraid that Mr. Breman would connect the talk of the rubber plants with his rubber factory, the factory with rubber stamps, and all the rest of his business. It was such a fatally smooth path; and the evening would be ruined. Or at least she would have to withdraw from it and go off by herself on a mental tour of other worlds. And Lyndall liked company.

But Breman's mind did not seem to run that way. "Did you notice in the Hotel the lady who wears an orange silk wig, and whose chin is held in place by an injection of parafine which would melt the minute she set foot in Algeria?"

Lyndall's husband asked him if he preferred the South American lady who sat on two chairs at once and could not see her little Pekinese when he curled up on her lap.

"No," said Mr. Breman.

"Would you prefer," asked Lyndall, "A lean modern woman who can throw undecipherable phrases at you at the same time as an unanswerable tennis ball?"

"My dream," said Mr. Breman, "is of a woman who could look pale and intellectual, wear very subtle dresses, listen to music with the expression of Da Vinci's Saint Ann; who could serve tea with deft hands, make ironic remarks . . ."

"Not so hard to find."

"Wait, that is not all. She must at the same time be able to walk tirelessly through mountain roads, in a plain little woolen suit, and have tan cheeks, a cheerful whistle, and a naive conversation."

Lyndall looked quite overwhelmed with this description and answered with a long silence. "It's too novelistic a wish," she said at last.

"I write in my spare time," said Mr. Breman.

"Oh," said Lyndall's husband, "I now understand why the conversation was getting off the logical sphere. I thought it was the Riviera night, the plants, and the sea."

They could hardly see each other's faces now. Fragrance from other plants came hovering over them. The waves lapped very gently. The cigarettes gleamed like fireflies.

"I'm also a fake businessman," added Lyndall's husband after a moment. "I prefer biography to economics."

"He makes this confession only in the dark," said Lyndall.

"It's too bad I must leave tomorrow," said Mr. Breman. "Tomorrow morning at nine. Business. And then to tell you the truth, I'm afraid of Nice. It's a tricky place. It takes the sting out of existence. I talk against it to keep myself awake, so to speak. The truth is that it enchants me, lulls me, makes me look down on all the big things I build up, makes me despise activity. And have you noticed that the people who are sunning the last years of their lives here try to keep you, offer you their guest rooms, sun porches, and yachts? After a while I don't feel that I am walking but riding on clouds; all the harsh sounds disappear, all sense of struggle, and all desire. It's a Hindu philosophy you get here — desirelessness, annihilation . . ."

"It's restful," said Lyndall's husband. "Accept it as such, and then when you feel energetic again, get out."

"But then I never do."

"So it's because you are afraid of Nice that you are leaving so suddenly."

"Yes." He tapped his side pocket. "I have my ticket here."

The three of them got up and walked leisurely back to the hotel. In the elevator Lyndall's husband remembered he had no cigarettes and he always smoked before going to bed. He stepped out. Lyndall and Mr. Breman stood there. Then he looked at her fully, with laughing eyes, and said: "It isn't Nice I'm afraid of, it's *you.*"

THE GYPSY FEELING

Mariette, help me. Is the first number finished?"

"The first number hasn't even begun. I've just been to see. The singer was called out twice and began a long, long encore. Don't you hear her?"

"Yes, damn her."

"You're not nervous?"

"Just a little — it's the first time I have danced in Paris — how do I know it will go well? Last night I saw a black cat crossing my path; you know what that means. And today is Friday. And Menuelo who has been running after that servant girl of mine. And Manuelito with the whooping cough . . . all these things worry me."

"Here are your carnations, and here are the combs."

"Give me the yellow ones first, now the red. I really look well today, eh? Mariette, you have no fire like me, but you're a nice friend. I never had a friend like you before." She turned to face her mirror, a warm, ample gypsy, with oily black hair, a fierce smile, and a dark gold skin. Her heavy breasts swelled and stretched the red bodice. "Help me with my shawl." She crossed and pinned it over her breasts. "Pull it down well at the back. I must show my back."

"It's a nice back you have," said Mariette. It was so well padded and curved down to her waist with soft sinuosity.

Lolita stamped her heels: "I mustn't forget to wet the soles of my shoes. Hold this candle will you?" She was carefully waxing her eyelashes. "Think of it, If I weren't dancing here I'd be at the factory, that's sure. With seven children you don't think I could afford to do nothing?"

Mariette played abstractedly with her fingers on the tambourine. She looked at her own fingers; they were quiet fingers. She looked at her face in the mirror; it was a quiet face. Where was her life? Certainly not on the *outside* of her; it was undetectable. Not as in Lolita overflowing in rich curves, meteoric eyes, nervous fat hands, shining hair, with some gold earrings always dancing around her face, some gold and coral necklaces rolling on her throat, or partly slipping down between the shadowed crevices of her polished breasts, to be nonchalantly pulled out warm and moist. For Lolita was always warm and moist, either from dancing or from fighting with Manuel, or from her last dinner, or from spanking one of the seven children. And from her body emanated a strong healthy animal odor. Everything could be seen in Lolita, felt and smelled. She made Mariette think of fat Spanish cakes swimming in fruit juice, of yellow Spanish candies melting like nectar in one's mouth, of the sun stirring in generous gold bodies an ever rising and spurting sap. Whenever in her work, in her solitary, quiet writing, Mariette suddenly ceased to feel her own body she had only to come and see Lolita to become all warm again.

Lolita's dress was rustling, with the windy undulations of multiple frills. Her many petticoats were perky with starch. With a billowing like a huge wave she passed out of the small dressing room, expanding with her own warmth, while Mariette shivered in the drafts in the theatre alley ways.

Mariette stood now between the folds of the grey curtain where she could see Lolita dancing.

Lolita dancing. And Mariette making up the words as she followed the gestures:

body straightened proudly, triumphantly for a minute and then a slow walk, a swift turn, and the drumming of feet — turn on the waist, arms waving overhead — slow undulations — one stamp — slow undulations — stamp, with the left arm curving around the head — and then riotous dancing with feet, body and

arms all at once, with beating of the tambourine . . . sudden
throwing forward of the breasts, an offering, feline gliding away,
undulations, fluid spirals, sudden snapping turn, abandonment . . .
swirls, maddening swirls. Stop. A slow languid walk, hips swinging,
swinging gently, legs opening . . . arms curling and uncurling with
joy, spiral movements of the body, turn and swirl — a stamp, neat
and firm — and a climax of stamping and drumming with the
rippling of the tambourine.

Or, for the second dance: a low crouching and sudden leaping
with jungle swiftness, savage running forward, with jerks and
spasms — shaking of all the body to the drumming of the feet,
blissful shaking to a climax of sudden stillness, with eyes phosphorescent green like those of animals in the dark, and a smile of knowing
intimate triumph, for the blood of the audience has caught up with
her rhythm and they too are panting with ardent joy . . .

It was over.

Combs, necklaces, earrings, flowers, starched petticoats, and
flame red dress were flung into a large yellow and red handkerchief.
Lolita put on a torn kimono and sat before the mirror, opening
her cold cream jar. Just then someone knocked. It was a big man
who stooped to get by the small door. He had the padded
shoulders and small waist of the 1931 model. Striped shirt and
broad trousers.

"Oh, Madame Lolita," he gasped. And stayed there. She
stretched her small fat hand. He bent over it and kissed it,
overwhelmed. "Your dancing." Lolita looked slowly at her cold
cream. The man took a three legged stool and sat there, with
admiration rippling from his eyes. Mariette threw a handkerchief
over the neck of Lolita so the young man would not see how
dirty the kimono was. Why she did that, she could not tell. He
was so young, and so excited by his vision.

Lolita, with a sigh, pushed the cold cream jar away, and
began to tie her bundle up and to put her street shoes on.
"Manuelo hasn't come," she said. "The old devil! Every time I
dance he takes advantage of it to take that girlie to a cafe. And
he the father of seven children. And I sweating away to support
him. Una vida de perro. Oh, well, husbands are like that." She sat
very quiet, her weight now sunken and nerveless after the dancing,
overflowing from the kimono.

"Meet my friend Mariette," said Lolita.

The young man gave a start, and stretched an awkward hand. "Are you a gypsy?" he asked.

"She writes," said Lolita, "she writes about dancing in newspapers." The young man turned his face away. "You know, I was overwhelmed with your dancing. It was so passionate, so full of gypsy emotion."

"Really," said Lolita, cleaning her nails.

"It was so lyrical! What fervor, what expressions. I was taken out of myself. I always had a dream about gypsies; to me, they are the only people who are *alive* in the world. I have looked for that gypsy feeling all over the world. Tell me how you live, tell me about your freedom, your feelings."

Mariette laughed.

"I don't know," said Lolita. "Manuelito has the whooping cough. That worries me. When I'm not dancing I have to cook and sew."

"Cook and sew! But you must hate it. What a come-down after the intensity and colorfulness of the dancing."

"Intensity yes," said Lolita. "I assure you it's damn hard work, but much more pleasant than the factory."

"Lolita has a lazy husband," said Mariette.

"Don't talk against him," said Lolita, "he's the father of my children. He owns a small farmhouse near Valencia. When we get old we'll retire there. I'm saving up for it. Days like today I'd like to be there already."

"But the thrill of your work, your fame," said the young man.

"It's a way of earning one's living. I've got to finish dressing."

The young man understood and left them.

Mariette took the bus home — to her hotel room. Her article must be ready for the next day. She worked at it until eleven-o'clock, going over the words that had come to her while watching Lolita dance. The typewriter ribbon had to be changed. Her quiet finger got impatient. I feel like dancing sometimes myself, she thought as she sat in her chair. She was in the theatre again, but not between the folds of the grey curtain. She was on the stage, undulating and stamping and beating the tambourine. She felt the old rhythmic sap beating inside of her. The sun, and the smell of animal skin, the taste of yellow Spanish candies, and the frenzied sun. And the description did not finish there. Mariette had suddenly a gypsy feeling: there were no more walls, no more boundaries, no thought. She ambled on in a tottering carriage, on the open road, and everything that happened happened without effort. She danced when she wanted to, slept when she wanted to, and dreamed, and washed her face and her clothes in the brooks, and talked with hoboes, and there was no worry about words but simply this enjoyment of being, all day on the open road, on friendly terms with curling and uncurling mists, skipping rain and the flicking and darling sunlight. And all the strength she gathered from the freshness and the solitude would burst into dancing, dancing to the rhythm of her own blood, and to the climax of her own emotions, and the extreme fullness of her body's power . . . dancing a gypsy feeling.

Oh, that typewriter ribbon which had slipped again. Anyway, the article was done. She was sleepy. She put the rubber cover on the last page, set her alarm clock early to reach the newspaper office, unpinned her very fuzzy hair and slipped her cool body through cool sheets — and damn the hotel maid who had forgotten her hot water bag.

There was, said the maid, a man waiting in the hotel parlor, (in that execrable green and purple room!). It was the young man who had called on Lolita. There was rapture on his face.

"You've got it, you've got it, the gypsy feeling! Pure! Perfect! Will you have dinner with me tonight?"

"What about Lolita," said Mariette.

"She's mending socks. By the way, did I tell you I was a poet?"

"I would have guessed it," said Mariette.

THE RUSSIAN WHO DID NOT BELIEVE IN MIRACLES AND WHY

She walked into a cafe on the Boulevard Montparnasse. The waiter mopped the little table. Next to her, facing a glass of cognac, sat a dejected looking young man, huddled on his chair.

"Coffee," she said to the waiter.

"Don't take coffee," said the man, "it's undrinkable. Give her some Porto, garcon." And when the waiter was gone: "I hope you have money to pay. I can't even pay my own."

"You'll be thrown out," she said.

"It's all the same to me. In a few hours I won't be alive."

She looked so startled that the man pulled himself together and leaned over his table to see her better.

"I'm Russian," he said, by way of explanation.

"Well?"

"I'm going to throw myself into the Seine when I leave this cafe."

"But why?"

"I'm through. No more money, and no more hopes of getting any." He turned away from her, gulped down his cognac, wiped his mouth with his sleeve. "At one time I had a palace . . ."

"I'll pay for your drink and lend you ten francs, but don't try and put any stories over on me."

"That's fair enough. Can you spare the money, though . . . you look . . . er . . ." His eyes were on her hat.

"What's wrong with me?" she said, taking off her hat and looking at it. "It just got wet."

"It probably looks better in dry weather," said the man. "This is hellish weather. The fog, particularly, upsets me."

"Oh, it upsets you too, does it?"

"Yes. And yet I like it. I like to imagine I have died, and then suddenly come into a new life."

"You could do that without dying. What stops you? I believe we can throw off yesterday's man like an old coat we don't want anymore, and actually enter into a new life. There are no walls between yesterday, today, and tomorrow, or between you and another life and another man. Try and see it everyday as you saw it today in the fog, a place where anything might happen. You don't know where your old home is so you might walk into a new one. You can't see the faces of the people you know, so you make friends with new ones, just as you did with me today. It is only an idea, the fear that today is related to yesterday, and that you cannot escape continuation. It is the fog which makes you see the world as it really is."

"I would like to change."

"Well, only desire it and it works like Aladdin's lamp."

"Then why," said the Russian, "don't you wish yourself another hat?"

She sulked for a while. The cafe was getting empty. The waiters were piling up the chairs and beginning to sweep. The Russian was brooding. He finally looked at her tenderly to appease her.

"Could you change your own life?" he asked.

"Of course I could. No plans are made. The world is a chaos. We take what we want, if we have enough nerve, and if we desire it ardently enough. You are here today because your head was blank."

"No, it was my pocket which was empty."

"The money is an excuse."

"It never comes."

"Go out and take it."

"I don't believe you. Why don't you wish something for yourself?"

"People who have good ideas have no time to try them out."

"What kind of life have you had?"

"Outwardly dull, but really exciting inside."

"Inside of what?"

"Of my own head."

"Where do you come from?"

"From everywhere. My blood is mixed. I have fed on books, mostly, so I'm top heavy, and a little dizzy."

"Would it be possible for a mousy person like you to become a dancer, for example?"

"Quite possible."

"How long would it take you?"

"Postpone the dying."

"I know a place where the coffee is good — Chez Bonhomme. Will you meet me there?"

"In a week, then."

"A week? But the ten france you gave me will only last me a day!"

"Aren't you going to change your life?"

"I don't know any women," said the Russian. "This year they are all for the Argentines and the Spaniards."

She postponed the meeting for many months. When she appeared at last in the cafe where they had first met, on a foggy evening too, he looked sullen.

"Champagne," she ordered boldly, shaking a beautifully hatted head with a new air.

"We might have met in a gayer place," said the Russian, sniffing the air to analyze the cost of her perfume. "You did it rather quickly. Who is it?"

"Just got some stage work."

"I'll pay your drink and lend you ten francs, but don't try and put any stories over on me."

She gave him a ticket to the show she was appearing in. She was in the chorus. "And how are you?"

"Me? All ready for the Seine again. After all, you don't really want to help me."

"Not with money."

"When you like somebody, why don't you help him out?"

"Why should I like you?"

The Russian looked dismal and offended. "I never made a catalogue."

The champagne filled in a blank moment.

"We have not much to say to each other," said the Russian dolefully. "I had better make love to you." He leaned over with his best technique of approach.

"Too easy," she said. "It's monotonous. For a change, the one woman you won't have. Isn't that interesting?"

"It's a game," he said. "The end is always the same."

"I see you believe in change . . . in changes of women. But that won't change *you.*"

"Do you think I need to?"

"Rather. But . . . goodbye!"

"Don't go. I like to hear you talk. Besides, listen to me. All this has happened to me once before, that is why it won't work. A woman asked me to change. I think women like that game. I was all alone, cold, flabby, pessimistic, indifferent. She watched over me; she was tender, she was sweet, she was strenuous. I, hearing what she believed of me, began to believe it too. It used to warm me up. It was a ressurection. She brought out all my talents. I had written some plays. She made me sell one, and then another. I made friends. She pushed me into everything. I began to walk airily, to laugh, to get witty, to come to life. She was happy. There she was, warming me up, injecting enthusiasm into me, with her words and her presence, and with promises . . . no, she never gave anything tangible. She held herself off like a distant goal. So, as I said, I became a success. I had forgotten the Seine. And then she ceased taking an interest in me. I was made. She was happy. But she had already picked up somewhere another unfortunate man, and was busy inspiring him. So you see, I decided to remain unfortunate. I thought it would be more fun for you to go on pitying me, understanding, having to understand, my distress."

He looked up expectantly at her.

"Oh," she said sadly, "now I know there is to be no miracle."

"You like miracles? That is too bad. You live on miracles, and I thrive on chronic pity. Yet this time I would rather lose the chance of getting another ten francs than to let you believe in fog, and the resurrection of desperate Russians."

"You don't believe in miracles?"

"No," said the Russian. "Because I was born in Place Clichy and I am not a Russian."

THE DANCE WHICH COULD NOT BE DANCED

He was standing in the deep violaceous shadow, a hermit, still and watchful, outside of life. Life was gathered around the fountain, in the sybaritic women carrying water, in the raising of their arms to sustain the jugs on their heads, in the sibilance of the water and the women's voices, and life was in the spiritous sunlight splintering the air to isolate shadows. He stood in the shadow, listening, and beneath the sound of water and the clangor of jugs and voices he heard other sounds, and beneath them still others perceptible to his divining ears, and all the sounds together rose up towards him, and all the sounds together had a rhythm which beat inside his head against the sides of his resonant mind, one layer upon another, unfolding, falling and rising, and the raising of the arms was a sound very clear to him, and the paradic sunlight was a sound, and the walking of the soft-fleshed women was a sound, heavy and persistent, and the falling of the water was not only the sound of falling water but the washing of the sea and of tears, and the sibilance of voices repeating all the words which had been spoken in the world, and all the feelings which made an unbearable resonance in his mind, all the cries, all washing against the resonance of his mind, divining one sound within another, eternally, as he divined one soul within another, one soul within another, and one dream within another.

The sounds rising in his mind burst their shell and split into black notes up and down black lines, black notes and white notes encroaching on each other, interplayed, interchanged, hooked, or

33

disconnected, toppling down and leaping up — ensorcelled out of his head into his hands, on paper.

"I will call it a dance," he said.

She was a sylphidine dancer, plied to music and to rhythm, and here was a dance for her, and she listened with impatient feet, ready for salutation, ready to bend and bow. She heard the rhythm well, she stamped her feet, and began, but could not enter into the song, could not follow it nor be lifted by it. Each step seemed like a counterstep to the beat of the music. "Play it quicker," she said to the pianist. "No, play it slower." Her feet could not find the undertone tread of the music. They stamped in discord, and then stood still. The refulgent song plied her, and there was a tremor in her, but not one she would dance with her feet. There was a tremor she would dance within herself, quietly, a movement she would keep within her body. She took her shawl off, and her flowers, and her earrings and bracelets, and she danced within herself from then on, hidden to human eyes, with a song and a joy and a rhythm no one could see but herself, and deeper and deeper she found in herself a fullness of measure she had not found until then. Whenever the dance was played, the feet stood still, and livingness ceased to be a jerking of muscles, a paroxysm of legs, and a wearing of shawls and of flowers, and the movement lay beneath the contortions and settled within, and living was not a marching and trumpeting and noise, but a continuous flowing of song underneath, a dance within a dance, a dream within a dream, stretching to infinity, with the perpetual cadence of inviolate dancing, inviolate living.

A DANGEROUS PERFUME

Lyndall was not very happy to be attending to business on a soft Parisian day, with her most becoming costume on. She was painfully aware that there were thousands of more interesting things to do than to see Miss Harney about the inventory of the apartment she had rented from her for six months. It was a month since she had moved out of it and the meeting had been delayed long enough; Miss Harney was growing terse over the telephone: "There are towels missing, and many things we must talk about."

Lyndall was too early for the appointment. Miss Harney let her in but asked her to wait while she finished dressing. Lyndall sat on the couch and observed that the apartment looked grey and quiet again. When she had occupied it she had enlivened it with vivid colored pottery, silk hangings and colored lamps. She looked absent-mindedly at her hands, and realized she was caressing the rough wool cover of the couch. She stood up suddenly, with a gesture as if throwing off something that annoyed her, and walked to the window. "I ought to be thinking about the towels," she murmured.

Miss Harney came in, with a well laundered appearance, impersonal eyes, and a firm handshake.

"Did my maid break many things? It's too bad. She was a clean little thing," said Lyndall, appealing to the impassible face.

"Very clean. But there is still a smell of perfume, and I always hated perfume."

"I never thought it would be so persistent. You might try ammonia."

Miss Harney took her list out of her desk, made Lyndall sit on the couch, sat in an armchair in front of her, and began to read it off: "Two face towels, two soup plates, and one of the glasses was chipped." Suddenly her voice broke and the paper trembled slightly in her hands. "Do you believe in intuition?" she asked, looking sharply into Lyndall's face.

"Of course!"

"I mean developed to a degree of divination."

"I do. But I never imagined you thought about it."

"You never understood me."

"I thought you were always scientifically inclined, and skeptical about the rest. You laughed at an experience Mr. Bowen told us about, right here, one evening, do you remember?"

"Yes, that is true."

Lyndall thought Miss Harney was asking idle questions, and would soon go on with the inventory. But instead she threw the list on the floor. "What's the use, you can never pay me back for what you have done to my apartment. I can't live in it anymore."

Lyndall looked startled. "What do you mean?" she asked sharply.

"Ever since you have lived here, my home is changed."

"I don't see anything changed. It looks as it always did. It looks like you. I did change it when it was mine, but there is no trace of that except the perfume."

"You don't understand. I *feel* strangely in it. I can't sleep at night. I have been here a month now. I thought it was the perfume, which evoked your presence so continuously. I thought of you every moment, and of your husband, and of *someone else.*"

"Of someone else?"

"Someone else who sat there next to you. Not your husband."

"I had many friends."

"I felt it was more than a friend."

"Miss Harney, you upset me very much. I don't know what you are talking about."

"You do know. It's queer how the perfume brought me the image of you in those splendid dresses you wear, of you with a strangely altered face, not as you look every day, for me, or in the street. It was a transfigured face. And when I saw you I sensed something very heavy, and dark, and unholy."

"You are dreaming! You are mad!"

"You know I am not. Something happened here, on that couch."

Lyndall sprang up, tense and pale. "I'm afraid you are not in your right mind."

"You know I am."

"You have been reading too many novels."

"I read nothing but philosophy."

"You have always hated me."

"Oh, *that* is true. Because you create around you a sort of misty and treacherous atmosphere. Everything about you looks beautiful. You have a gift for setting, for poses, and gestures, for clothing yourself. Your voice has a peculiar tremor, and your face is haunting. I feel all that myself. Imagine what men must feel!"

"Those are not reasons for you to hate me. And if you think I am loved for these things, why do you not acquire them too?"

"Never! It would always look unnatural, whereas in you it *seems* terribly sincere."

"Why should it not be sincere?" said Lyndall sadly. "I love beauty."

"You love beauty," repeated Miss Harney mockingly. "But what is beauty *for?* What do you love it for?"

"For it's own sake!"

"Oh, no, no," said Miss Harney bitterly. "For passion!"

"We have come back to the unholy mystery! What is it you imagine? That I am involved in love affairs?"

"I don't know quite what it is I feel. . . No. No ordinary love affairs. Something very intense and strange, which disturbs and stirs me. Don't think I merely envy you. I simply can't stand this feeling you have brought into my home. It is as if all you have touched gave out a kind of fever."

"And if it were . . . just . . . passion, why should you hate it so?"

"I don't hate it! I want it myself, Lyndall, just as it is around you, rich and heavy and warm, dissolving all those cool calculations I make to convince myself that it is not of great value. But since I cannot have it, I want my peace. You have destroyed my peace. Tell me, tell me, this man who came here, he loved you?"

"He desired me."

Miss Harney's eyes up to this moment hard and questioning, now turned away.

"Many times," said Lyndall slowly, "when we sat here, I could feel his excitement and he mine. It did not matter after a while what it was we talked about. Every word, we felt, could be the one before the climax. He delayed it on purpose. The waiting, the tremendous tension, the force of this impulse were wonderful to feel, in themselves. He was so sure I would yield. When we talked we let our hands lie near, and he did not touch me, but undercurrents, undercurrents of the most maddening sharpness flowed between us. Then when he kissed me, I knew he did not love me. I sent him away." Then Lyndall's voice hardened as she added: "I don't know why I should be talking about this."

"And it was only a kiss!" said Miss Harney softly.

"Some kisses," said Lyndall, "can explode the whole set plan of a life."

There was a moment of silence.

"I feel that I can live in this place *now*", said Miss Harney.

"Not I," said Lyndall.

RED ROSES

She wanted red roses, red roses. Not the mystical snow-flowers of her still dreams, the ones she unraveled in the silence of her room, the flowers of magnified snow-drops. That is what she desired most painfully, red roses. She could not wait patiently for them; they were the initiation flower to the blood dreams, they must come soon because she wanted them, they must obey her desire and not someone else's slow vision, the slowness of the world, slow to see that she was ready for the red flowers.

With the money in the palm of her hand, she walked down the hill to the village florist. She ordered red roses. She wrote her own name on the little card, her own address. She ordered them to be delivered very soon.

In order for them to be a surprise they must arrive when she was not expecting them. So she walked very fast back to the old house, and went to the cellar to look at the seeds growing there in boxes. The care of them kept her very busy, in this garden of darkness, a garden of little seeds sprouting with such fragility in the warmth of the cellar.

The doorbell rang when her hands were dirty. She rushed to wash them. She opened the door to the florist boy carrying the red roses in transparent paper. Red roses! And who had sent them? Leave them there. Thank you. In her impatience to see who sent them she cannot open the little envelope. At last. The words are printed. Of course. He bears no name yet. That is natural. But he brings the words: "From Your Lover." And the simple message is expanded a million times by the glow of the flowers.

It was all very beautiful. The snowy dreams were outside now, lying still in the form of a white carpet, all around the house. And inside was the flame, many little flames offered to her. What could one do with flowers? The pleasure was too great; it gave her a fever. The pleasure could not end in the simple act of placing them in water. The initiation roses, marking the moment of hasty rhythms, the end of immobility. You are now a woman. Someone looked at you. Someone saw you. Someone worshipped. The house is so poor. The bannister is falling down. There are stains on the wall. The red roses are prodigal, extravagant, incredible here. The room is cold. The fire in the fireplace is not lit. The roses are lit like a bush of flames. And the more she looks at them the greater grows the flame in them and in her. The red roses are flames, addressed to the flame in her. She cannot place them in a vase. She is overflowing with their redness. Not flowers, not flowers but the red key word to the new worlds of fire. They will burn the house, they will burn down the house, and melt the snow, and burn her and all her brothers and sisters, her mother, her father, the neighbors. They will burn the village, and spread in circles throughout the whole land and scar the city. She takes them in her arms. She runs away from the house, as if to save them all from the conflagration. She carries them running to the Church. The Church opens its yawning caverns. It will not burn. For centuries the candlelight and the flames of watch lamps burn in her bowels without danger. Flowers and candles perpetually offered in sacrifice. She could add her red roses to them, the red roses sent by man to the virgin, given to the virgin, as an offering, of secret joy, and abdication.

I give back to God what He sent me, I am grateful, thankful, grateful for the gift. I give you back what was given me. Hear my prayer. I wanted red roses. Perhaps it was wrong. But if I offer them to you, it is not wrong. Take them. I am a woman. The woman was given red roses. They burn me. Now they burn for you. But I still have the joy, this joy of being woman. I am woman, such a joy I cannot hold. Hear my prayer. I cannot pray. It is the joy. Take the joy. Is it wrong? Here is my joy and my red roses, but I cannot be as I was yesterday, before they came. I will never be as I was yesterday. Was it wrong? Take the roses, and my gratitude, and the joy, it is too much for me, all in one day. I cannot bear it when my desires are fulfilled.

OUR MINDS ARE ENGAGED

They met after eight years of separation. They looked at each other intently. Who are you now? An abyss, over which they looked affectionately, drawn by a persistent obsession with memories.

"Do you remember, the first day I saw you you were about fifteen — I came from college with my brothers. We stood in the hallway of the house. You came out of a dark room — very fragile, intensely pale, with huge frightened deer-eyes, and you said in a timid voice: 'My mother is out.' My brothers talked and I merely looked at you. Afterwards, you had confidence in me. You took me up to a room where you were working on the presentation of a play. You showed me the costumes you had made out of cheese-cloth, and Christmas tree ornaments, and bedspreads and curtains. In that room you talked — as long as it concerned plays, and all that. You liked me because I fixed the curtain for you. Do you remember?"

"Yes, I remember. And then your letters from college, and the boxes filled with flowers you gathered in the woods."

"And the terrible poetry."

"And the sentimentality: you were an angel, a goddess, a saint, to be worshipped, and never touched."

"And the pale, poetic, delicate intensity."

"Awful!"

"And now?"

Again they looked.

He was thirty now, slow-mannered, with supple, feline gestures, a lavish voice, a persuasive way of using his hands, a talent for silences.

Again she was asking him to take a part in her play. Her play was now her very life; her house, carefully arranged as an absolutely fitting background to her imaginative costumes. Immediately, on that love of the play, there would come intimacy. But the difference was there was nothing he could fix; there was nothing in which she showed any helplessness. He was a little disappointed.

They still looked at each other.

"In what world are you now?"

Suddenly he observed in the library, six books by D.H. Lawrence. They found themselves in the same world, in Lawrence's world, he who had created a language and a symbolism, and a universe of feelings. Through his own language they talked now, using words in his own way, asking each other the questions he asked, finding no answer.

"How do you live?"

"By what philosophy do you live?"

"Oh, the philosophy is alright, it is easy to get, but impossible to stick to."

"Why?"

"You remember our sentimentalism?"

"I don't want to remember it."

"It was the first sign of an excess of feeling. This excess of feeling has now gone into good acting, and good writing. It has become the very precious element of intensity, by which alone one fulfills life. But . . ."

"We topple over."

"Yes. But in you, it is not destructive. In me . . ."

"Before you came, I heard that you had been in love."

"With Ella, yes. I have thought I was, and before her I thought I was in love with . . . and before that . . ."

"Yes, I remember, it was always like that."

Between them now stood an idea they would not put into words: "If we had been lovers, perhaps, it might have changed the course of his life."

His eyes reproached her. "Perhaps, if at that moment of my

awakening you had not been such a phantom, other people might not have seemed more real. *He* seemed so much more human."

"Why were you not more human? Why did you never touch me? I really wished you would."

"You did not show it. Your face shone distantly, with detachment; your hands were always excessively busy. We were so intensely connected by dreams."

"Who did you really love? Wholly?"

"He was a very talented, a very brilliant person."

She was very sad after their talk. Inchoate, tragic struggles, heavy; they oppressed her, she who had always tried to clarify and lighten him. She sensed that her clarity was useless — it was thought; he had to bear revelations through feeling. Her own energy was useless to him; he must find his own power. She could not help him. She could only listen.

On the velvet pillow of the divan he marked a circle. Life was to him like the edge of a bowl. He had begun at the center of the bowl with the ideas taught to him of what he should feel and do. Then the circumference widened, pushed out by his personal discoveries and instincts. He enlarged and enlarged the horizon of his acts. He went to the very edge of the bowl and fell out of it — with Gide, Proust, and perhaps Da Vinci. He exhausted his physical impulses, and then returned. He did not want that climax. He had been aware in himself of all the strange desires that could be felt on this earth, but to fulfill them was not to fulfill his dreams. He was in destructive conflict. What he desired was wholeness and normalcy, through the love of woman. To be made to feel whole, entire, man.

She listened.

"Talking to you has helped me to forget my misery. Today I received a letter from him."

She summoned with her mind all the strength of her understanding. She must have watchfulness and divination. She was not afraid of pain, only afraid of being woman, of clinging. Clinging did not make such men feel whole.

"Sometimes," he said, "when I was drunk, I felt in harmony with the world, and quite entire. Sometimes when a whore appealed to me, I thought I had at last grasped a closeness to woman through which I might realize ultimate passion. It was only a spark. I would soon fall back again, and the first moment of lucidity would bring back the intolerable splitting. I was so drawn to him, and yet conscious of the immaturity, the incompleteness of my instinct."

He did not like irony, though he was amused by hers.

"But irony is a form of lucidity," she said, "it is a cooling off of the mind." (What elation, to disagree.)

"Lawrence was not an artist in the strictest sense of the word. His prose should have been poetry."

"No," she said. "He made new prose, lyrical prose with the intensity of poetry."

"But it is not all artistic."

"In parts it is perfect poetic prose, just as perfect as poetry."

"I don't believe in poetic prose — I believe in poetry."

"I believe in poetic prose. I am doing it."

"I believe in poetry. *I* am doing it. And by the way, you must help me find a studio. I have to work on the illustrations."

He kissed her hand. Irony helped her here. She smiled indulgently, responsive but not inflammable, or if, inflammable, not explosive.

"It's funny," he said, "you do not ask me to love you one hundred percent. All women ask me to love them one hundred percent."

"An unimaginative request. A woman will come who will not demand to be loved one hundred percent."

"Who is she?"

"She is a woman in my last story, my ultra modern woman who is busy with her own visions and her own work."

"Oh," he said, but that is the woman I do *not* want. I seek a peasant woman, the earth-woman, the primitive, vulnerable, docile woman."

"Why do you talk to me?"

"Because I can't talk to the peasant woman — and also because you're really the person I *want* to love. And yet I have the presentiment that I will lose you again through my own fault. It is terrible."

And then moods, black moods, all wisdom and all courage scattered. She had said she did not mind, let them enjoy the present. She did not mean what she said. For a moment they were so curiously, so strangely tuned to the same feelings, both finding out truths with the same plodding sincerity, the same self-forgetfulness. So rare, that sameness of mind, always the right answer, the immediate response, the continuation of one's own dreams, mixtures of dreams which led on to fecund phantasies.

Sitting at a cafe table, they observed that they were both busy with the same slow, integral development, step by step, solid and complete.

They were both saying: "I want to be alone and to work," yet they lingered at the cafe table, face to face, although their talk brought nothing but pain and restlessness. Talking about their desire for connection with life through love and through creation, when all the while they wished a connection between themselves.

"There is only a possibility of perfection in art, which is solitary," she said.

He did not contradict her.

Warm, brilliant morning. They set out to look for his studio. She wore a light green dress and light green hat. She was gay and light, free and clear minded.

He felt the lightness and was suddenly delivered of his own heaviness. He said: "I love your insousiance."

The atmosphere was suddenly cleared up, there was no more malaise. She asked nothing; he gave what he could give. She looked fearlessly and quietly into his face and he was grateful for the fearlessness and the quietness. His confidence came back. He took her arm. And how they talked! There was to be an artistic fulfilment; he would illustrate her mystical stories. They dreamed about that. Art, art, was a fulfillment.

The day is bright and warm, the bus shakes them — she is light, so light.

Where is that brooding intensity and heaviness which had weighed down their relationship? She had dissolved it. It is all crystal clearness now, man to man, almost.

What of the pale green dress and bare ivory arms, and coral bracelet and his hand on her arm, and his green eyes, and the sensuousness of his face and walk? Delight, delight, and nothing more. His freedom, her freedom. She carried a world, and therefore did not demand one from him.

"Go, my dear, go," she said.

"I can stay, then," he says, elated by the strength in her. And she smiles, because he did not see her yesterday.

He moved into his studio. She went with him, made his bed, hung up his clothes while he unpacked and they went shopping together. They nailed a nail with one of his shoes and played at the beginning of his bohemian life, and then went to the Dome for coffee.

Then he said: "Have men ever told you that they wanted to destroy you? Well, I feel like that. You obsess me. The mental connection between us obsesses me. I cannot stop thinking about it. I know I shall never find anything like it in the world. I know that would be the ideal. *I want to love you.* I wish we had never begun by that mental connection, I wish we had never begun by dreaming together, for now I cannot touch you, there is a veil between us. I want to touch you, to grasp you in another way than the mental and I long for that and yet I cannot do it. I fear to lose you, and I won't be satisfied with that fulfillment in art we talked about. I don't want any half measures; either everything or nothing; this connection between our ideas and feelings is too obsessive."

As they sat there the physical current was so slight, more like a tremor. She knew he would never touch her, and that even if he touched her he could never hold her. So she savoured the hot sound of his voice dropping so low, as if to penetrate her: "I *want* to love you." She savoured the way they sat, shoulders touching, she quite aware of the contact, quite aware of the caress of his eyes on the outline of her body, aware of the slight, unreal tremor in himself, a tremor of the mind, a passion of the mind — a mere craving.

She lived that moment a whole long life with him. There would be tenderness and sharpness, a feeling of satanic and elusive beauty, unreachable, untouchable, unreal feelings, always falling short, something always falling short, thin, evanescent, teasing, incomplete — just that feeble call to living: I *want* to love, in a low, tormented voice.

Strange that this cool stillness should hurt itself by creating cool stillness around it. She sat next to him, now profoundly still, as if enchanted by a curse — an unknown poison filtering through her veins . . . as if men and women's tremendous craving to melt into one another, and to become one, had indeed been fulfilled in a diabolical manner; man and woman, indeed, in *one* . . . in Him.

One day he came very near loving her. They were leaning over Blake's poetry, in the park. She felt that he was moved.

And then he went on with his botany lessons:

"I think it is terrible of you not to know the names of trees."

"Why should I?"

"Because you make a friend of it. This tree, for instance, is a platane. You come and say: 'Hello, platane.' It's more familiar."

"But perhaps even though it is a platane it may have the feelings of some other kind of tree? Why pigeonhole him like that?"

"That's true. This platane has the character of an oak."

But he went on: "This is a locust tree, this is a birch."

He had lost two buttons off his shirt and his chest was bare. And she did not feel towards him as towards a man with a bare chest. She felt nothing. His face shone with extraordinary intensity, his eyes took on all the shades of the foliage and the lake. His head was constantly tilted upward, as if he were looking into the face of the sun, with full, frank sensuality in his mouth. How could so much brightness be cold rather than warmly living?

When she was sharing the sandwiches they had brought he said: "You could get away with a great deal of modernism. You answer Lawrence's description of the woman who is at once cocksure and demure. If you were only cocksure you would be impossible."

There was a moment of silence.

"What are you thinking of?" she asked.

"You know, *he* had the most attractive way of being always over-eager about everything, always full of curiosity and interest. I used to enjoy getting a great many ideas out of books and bringing them to him, to see the eagerness with which he grasped them."

"Did you get another letter from him?"

"Yes."

"Is he also unhappy?"

"We are going through a great struggle, both of us."

"Will you ever see him again?"

"When we are both very strong."

"Read me his letter."

He read it to her.

"It is very beautiful," she said, "almost classical in tone, so restrained and so intelligent."

"I'll read you Minnie's letter."

"It sounds like a dime novel," she said. "Who was she?"

"She is the person I tried to fight him with."

"Why do you oppose an inferior to him?"

"A superior man can inspire harmonious love in me, but I cannot love women who appeal to my intellect. Listen, I wrote a poem to St. Anne and to you."

It was strainge to hear him speak of his own deadness with lyrical intensity — strange how he could make poetry out of it. Sitting beside him, she felt again that deadness enfolding her, and herself becoming a St. Anne, not in the foreground like the Mother who lives in the child, but in the background, having finished with life, now dispensing understanding, herself entire, wise, aware of everything, savouring the poetry of his resplendent death and the possibility of his resurrection.

"Tell me more about him," she said.

She tried to work, when alone, but she could not work well. There was in human relationships a physical pain, aside from any intellectual control — a recurrent, unexpected, pain. She had the desire to see him, continuously, like a gnawing hunger. She was working; her head was busy, yet all the while she was conscious of physical pain, in the veins, in the blood, in the flesh.

She thought of a phrase of Christopher Morley's: "Our minds are engaged." Let us announce that our minds are engaged. But the body revolted. The St. Anne detachment did not last. She felt now hard, now soft.

All the while, the physical images looked in harmony. People noticed them in the street, eyes lingered on their two faces. People had felt they were bound. And now that he enjoyed the eccentricity of her costumes he liked to show her off, and took pleasure in people's thoughts that they were lovers.

Today she wanted everything definitely settled, even the relief of a break.

They met, both of them brisk, tense, discussing hotly about other things so as not to become conscious of their feelings — her recoiling and shivering — his insufficiency.

"I must find my peasant woman," he said. She felt that the one who cannot feel blames the other unconsciously. Even though he was very truthful he built up unconsciously a false image of her as a justification; an image of an over-intellectual person, seeing her split and fancying a separation where there was none because there was a separation in himself. He was building up a philosophy against women like her who were too strong for him. She did not mind his misunderstanding her but she minded his building up a false philosophy: intellectual women have not the nature of the true woman and therefore they do not bring out the maleness in man, they have weakened man. In other words today's woman was responsible for men like him.

He wrote a poem of such symbolical vastness that he startled many people. When his little book came out with the illustrations it showed how strong were his lyrical and visionary impulses. It was the moment of his ascension, a meteoric moment. He had fixed into poetry the struggle of his universe, and innumerable echoes answered him.

His own rich personal intensity broke its own shell and its own obsessions and touched the universal.

She was again vivified by his outburst. How he sang to the very phantoms which pursued him. His poetry swelled with impersonal intensity, it was a rich cascade of resonances. And the words fell all around her in splintered lightning with profound brightness. All this surrounded her, the poetry spoken in his own very pliable, very deep searching voice, the hypnotic words, the hallucinating rhythms, like the very rhythms of life, and then his gestures, flung out, even the simplest with the soft sureness of perfect instinct.

She followed with a pleasure which brushed the whole surface of her skin, like a wind, his walk towards her when they met. It was not as if he were walking up to a certain material barrier, a yard before her, or up to the cafe table, but as if urged by some profounder rhythm walk on with soft sureness through all visible barriers into some intimate and secret realm of her self. And so he walked, deliberating, stood or talked, persuasive, absorbing, with changing face, changeable ideas, changeable eyes, varying, and colored, heightened by all that persuasive feline power.

The brightness, the lyrical song quality of his acts and work and voice and manners was always disturbing, frustrating, raising a tremor in the flesh.

People would say he had charm.

She rented an old villa out in the country, for her moments of intensive work. It needed painting badly. She began with a small attic room. When she talked about it, he wished to help her.

She gave him an apron, and put one on herself. She wore odd clothes, and garden gloves.

"You are disguised as a peasant woman, now," he laughed, while she mixed the paint.

"You look primitive too, in your half grown beard."

They would eat lunch in the village, with the gardeners and workmen. He carried books in his pocket but did not talk about them. In the evening they would take the train home.

Working side by side they reached a new realm. In her homely old clothes she was stripped of artificiality and therefore of the attributes of her new life, self-made and unfamiliar to him. She looked much more like the deer-eyed girl he had first known.

And so in that little room, with its low attic roof and small window, he suddenly loomed larger and tyrannical, and she seemed to grow pliable and small. In an explosion of frankness he confessed: "I do not want to accept you as a sybilline woman, but as one who must grow all over again with me from the very beginning. I repudiate the woman you have become."

"But the woman I have become makes you a much better friend!"

But she was amused by his demands. She realized he was struggling to find his own image of her for his own exclusive possession.

He went on, trying to tumble down all that was already there, her new maturity, her sharpness, her writing, in order to mould her to something which would fit into his life and plans — the passive, uncreative woman.

He criticized her sharply because he thought she had been too much loved and spoiled and he wanted to treat her differently to impose his own opinions and standards.

He said: "I want you to be more real with me. He did not mean more real but more subject to his own evaluations.

They stopped painting, with the brushes held up in the air, and drops of rose paint falling down, unheeded.

She was explaining that she was willing to reject all she had achieved and to begin again if he really thought she had made false progress. It was the wiser woman, she knew, who kept finely balanced a most intricate relationship. Yet she understood that he should not enjoy a wisdom gained without him.

He was conscious at last of wanting her to yield to a symbolical assertion of himself, and she conscious of the deep joy of yielding. She would love nothing better than to begin life all over again with him, that they should find wisdom together.

And so she lay all her old wisdom aside, her experiences, her memories, her sureness, her creative work, and made herself small and docile — renunciating all he would discard.

He took up his painting again and sang to cover up his perplexity, for now that he had asserted himself and she had yielded, she did not know what else to do, since it was all a dream, a mystical venture without human plenitude.

And she also took up the painting again, face turned away, to conceal her triumph at having been conquered.

At the bus stop, where each was going his own way, he generously conceded: "After all, you were sybilline today."

She gathered herself together in a profound stillness. Every gesture and word and attitude was one of soft assimilation. But he made no use of the softness he encountered.

A strange light gathered in his eyes, as he watched her. She had covered her vivid personal world from his eyes — she seemed to have even silenced the bright activity of her inventions and fantasies. Her talk was a constant divination of his moods, and a worship of them.

He was becoming conscious of his incapacity to love her as a woman, and the pain of it shot out sharply. Out of his dark broodings came a long sequence of tormenting phrases and arguments, and taunts.

"How can you be entirely mine if you have a world of your own inside of your head and will not give it up? How can you love my work if you also love your work?"

Unexpectedly she realized his tyranny was not that of a lover but of the one who cannot love. She realized he wanted to make himself feel strong by making her weaker.

She had been so eager to help him find a philosophy she had not minded that he should build one which should destroy her, nor did she mind if his redemption was a repudiation of all she had been, was, and would continue to be. But seeing him build up this false strength she realized that her weakness did not make him really strong — that he felt strong only because he had the power to torment.

He was obsessed with his own incapacity to possess what he admired, to dominate and to hold, so he cried: "Be small, be creepy, warm, and mindless, that I may feel my own strength." He did not know it was the man who reached and plied whatever he desired — not the woman who had to squat.

She would not squat. She was tired of a man who could fear a woman's strength. She reentered her own world with joy. Wide horizons, air, space — how sweet the freedom.

She told him to go to the devil.

He bruised himself against her new mood, and was elated.
"How wonderful," he said; "to find a match in you!"
She had found it rather tiring. It had required a deep effort.
"I feel so attracted to you, just at this moment."
But she was entrenched in her own world. Already, when he had spoken the words, he had looked afraid that she might believe him.

They were walking together like good friends. She bore the burden of his confidences.

"There is a woman," he said. "She is a painter."

She looked at his elusive sensuous face, his feline body. She saw him hovering around this other woman, hovering, and being so appealing, so gentle, so charming, so cruel, so difficult. She saw her changing to suit his moods.

She said to him: "Try and not hurt her."

But she knew he would hurt her. It gave him such deep pleasure. It was the only pleasure he had — with women.

But the pleasure was unimportant. What was important was the convergence of all feelings in him, making him ultimately self sufficient, and the self-sufficiency in her because of the preponderance of the artist, so that wisdom awoke in both in spite of the non-human experience. She saw the symbolical plenitude in him, craving companionship only at moments, and he saw the symbolical plenitude in her, wavering only at moments. The awakened wisdom gained in sharpness because they had both carved out all personal softness and pain away from themselves, to gain an understanding of something nobody had cared to understand because of the fear of solitude.

ALCHEMY

The bell was rung so vehemently that the maid slipped and fell once on her way to answer it. She opened the huge iron gate breathlessly. The police dog announced the visitors with an exasperated howl.

"Is this where the 'great writer' lives?"

"Yes," said the maid. "Come in."

One of the visitors said: "I knew it must be here. I recognized the gate which he described so minutely in *Desperate Caravans.*"

"And yet," said another visitor, "it is not quite the same gate. Observe this one carefully; it is turquoise green, yes, but it is slender and formal. Whereas look at the neighbor's gate; it is grey, but notice the shape of it — it is smaller, slightly uneven, it has a squatty, secretive appearance. Now if you recollect the exact description in the book: '. . . it was a turquoise green gate with a secretive, squatty appearance . . .' "

"Come this way," said the maid.

"I think I recognize the servants too," said another visitor. "You remember in *Trembling Walls,* the girl who waited in the roadhouse was freckled and wrinkled, although young, and had exactly the same mousy manners . . ."

"But she had at the same time the most startlingly beautiful voice. He made a great point of the voice — a whole page — but this girl's voice is muffled."

Just then another maid appeared and called out in a limpid mielodorous* voice: "The great writer said you could come into his library."

There they were received by the "great writer's" wife who dispensed hospitality with a religious air. She had a very worn, very bored manner. She could not be the woman he constantly described as phosphorescent. At the same time she had a curious, sharp way of questioning the visitors which made them grow intimate and confiding in a few minutes.

"You see," explained the eldest, "we have all been reading your husband's work for three years, every book which has come out. We became eager to find out who the characters were supposed to be in real life, and where were the places he described. We have followed all possible leads. We have even suspected that he described himself in *Inundated Cellars.* Finally we decided to come and talk it over with him. It is so much simpler than to do so much guess work. Do you think he would mind?"

"I do not think he would mind," said the wife, "but I am afraid he would not tell you anything. You see, he is not very sociable; in fact, he never sees anybody. I am the one who goes visiting."

"Impossible!" exclaimed one of the visitors. "Why, he is the writer who is known to have produced the richest and most varied gallery of characters."

"Yes, he is good at that," said the wife.

"How does he do it?" they demanded in perfect unison.

"Take me for instance," said the wife. "I have served as a model for Anne, Mirabel, and Cynthia. For Anne he reproduced my way of firing direct and impossible questions. Only he put on me a face he had seen on a wax mannequin in a show window. He dressed 'me' up in a way suggested to him by an article against eccentric costumes. And thus Anne began, and by the end of the book she turned out an impossible, devastating personage. And you can see that I . . ."

"We can see," said the visitors gently.

"With Cynthia it was another thing. I used to talk a great deal about my girlhood. I described it entirely to him, pictured the

---

*Mielodorous: A word of doubtful alchemy from laboratory of J. Joyce

background, analyzed the characters of my parents, sketched pictures of the people who came to see us, of my teachers, read him my youthful journals, showed him the books I used to read and what I marked in them. He went suddenly ahead and wrote the exact opposite, a different background, a different girl, different circumstances, and parents. Everything I had said had suggested a contrary. Cynthia is a remarkable character, don't you think?"

"Very true to life," said one of the visitors.

"Of course, a description of *you* might have been equally remarkable," said the youngest and most susceptible visitor.

"Well, it occurred to him after a while, and it was then he wrote Mirabel."

"But Mirabel is not like you in the least!"

"I don't know," said the wife. "He wrote Mirabel with the intention of making a perfect likeness. It was wonderfully begun. There was my tired air, my sophisticated boredom, my airy hair, and my way of thinking aloud. But then when it was all put down he realized it was inconsistent for a queer person like Mirabel to marry a man like himself. He explained it all to me. He said: 'Take two persons like that, both intelligent and both analytical, make them live together. Why, they would spend all their time analyzing each other's emotions until the emotions would be dried up. And it would be harassing to describe such analysis. I must give Mirabel a man with impulses and intuition but without consciousness.' And so he did. And when Mirabel married this man she naturally became a different woman, and by the end of the book she was quite beautifully intuitive and natural, with a youthful enthusiasm for inept living. And so there you have Mirabel."

"Remarkably true to life," said one of the visitors.

"But why does he make his wives always so uncomprehending," said the youngest visitor, "if you . . ."

"Very kind of you to realize that I *do* understand. But I can explain that. The most extraordinary event in my husband's life was an illicit passion he experienced for a very uncomprehending woman, a lovely woman. The excitement of trying to keep it all a secret from me (I would not tell him I knew because I would not spoil his fun) the torment of being pulled now here, now there, the novelty of feeling pernicious and unbalanced, powerful and dangerous, were the most stimulating emotions he had ever known.

When he outgrew the woman, he retained the emotions, but in transferring them into a book he allied them to his feeling for my comprehension, and by this alchemy obtained a certain intensity and maturity of experience which he afterwards often used, and was many times inspired by. But then in the books this combination of comprehension and passion, to remain properly heightened, was given to the character of the mistress, and his old mistress became the model for the wife. And there you are."

"Marvellously true to life," said one of the visitors who was embarrassed and did not know what else to say.

"It was not true to life when it was written," said the wife, "but it became true to life afterwards, for many people who read that book began to discover such feelings in themselves, and so began to look around for a mistress."

"And what about his marvellous feeling for children? How did he get that?"

"We have a little white poodle." said the wife, "He is the most adorable, the most affectionate and naughtiest thing you ever saw. My husband bathes him, brushes his hair, plays ball with him, and he has often said: 'I can understand the feeling that a baby can give you. Just look at him, the helpless, cute way he is looking at me, lying on his back, with his small tender paws stretched innocently towards me.' "

The wife then gave the visitors some autographed copies of the great writer's last book, and walked with them to the gate.

When they looked back at the house they saw a scarf of smoke waving over the chimney.

"He is mixing his ingredients," they said.

TISHNAR

Paris was wrapped in a white fog. It had receded into deep shadows and become impalpable. Faces surged up before her unexpectedly but remained vague. She met black shadows which might be men of other times. All sounds were muffled and strange. She walked on hazy streets without ends and turned corners which led into flying mists. She saw books in their boxes, extended halfway on the sidewalk and could not read their names. The little cafe tables were in her way too, but empty and wet. She was isolated from the rest of the world and homeless. Her face seemed vague to others, her figure was like a shadow and her voice without echo and warmth, and her eyes had lost their brightness and her walking was like a glide, soundless and dead.

She had sought such a moment throughout the world, where she might be quite alone, where no one might read on her face thoughts she could not hide; where no one could plainly notice her walk was slow and sad, and miss the sound of her step when she could not walk any longer; a place where she might be forgotten and lost. She had sought to stand on the edge of another world, where her voice would make no warm sound, where her steps should not be heard, where she could follow streets without end, and see with lusterless eyes a life that could not be touched and felt like our own.

The rain on her face was real, and the wind on her back, but what was the spirit that moved her? And why should the sound of real voices startle and frighten her? She liked to be alone with the rain on her face, and the fog, and the wind on her back. The people who laugh should pass her by, and so with the people who talk. She sought a world without color and sound, where no one might notice her fingers locked on dreams, and her eyes which saw nothing but shadows.

The fog had lifted very slowly, like a very old curtain in a very old playhouse. She found herself standing by the bus stop, with a little ticket in her hand, and many people waiting their turn with her.

The bus was very full and started running laboriously away from the Opera, creaking, and sliding and jogging. The rain was whipping about, swishing, and beating the ground. People sat staring at each other and at the dripping windows. There was a smell of umbrellas, and rubber, and wet wool and leather, and cigars and cheap perfumes.

The lights in the bus gleamed yellow and pale. Dull eyes were staring back and forth, staring out of huddled bodies.

Nobody was getting off.

The conductor stood in the corner of the platform, with his collar turned up. On and on, with squeaks, with sudden turns to evade other cars, with sudden languors when travelling up hill, the bus ran away from the Opera.

Nobody was getting off. The conductor had put up the sign: "Complet." The bus was passing by all the streets she knew, passing them quickly and carelessly, and more people stood sheepishly under the lamplights with the rain dripping down their faces. She stood up and ran to the platform. She could not find any bell . . .

"Please," she said to the conductor, "Will you stop for me?"

"This bus never stops," said the man. "You must have made a mistake . . . in the fog perhaps. People often do. We make this trip only once . . . Didn't you see the sign in the front?"

"What does it say?"

"Another world," said the conductor.

"But I don't want to go there," she said, "not really. It was only a wish, only a wish . . . I want to go back to the Opera. Do let me get off. Look, there are so many people waiting there to take my place."

Just then someone ran after the bus, and jumped on the step and hung on the strap for a minute. She saw the face she had long carved in her mind and wanted to find and to love all her life.

"Complet," cried the conductor angrily, pushing him off and ringing his bell wildly for the bus to go on.

And the man was left standing in the middle of the street, with the rain pouring down his face while he looked at her.

THE IDEALIST

From the very first day Edward knew they were drawing the wrong person. The whole class was turned towards the model who had been chosen for them, a woman with a very brown body who, from the waist down seemed heavily rooted to the ground by a sort of sinking of her flesh, a strong implantation of her feet on the model stand, a heavy droop of her arms and shoulders. But the woman he was looking at and drawing surreptitiously was poised before him with such an air of having stopped only a minute here on her way to something else that he immediately began to think of ways of speaking to her for fear she might not be there the next day. Her face was tranquil, and her eyes virtuously concentrated on the model, and her fingers were correctly drawing what she was looking at, but even then he felt such a restlessness in her, such a self-sufficiency, as if she carried her own world within her and did not need to cling to any group, or place.

"I hope you will come again tomorrow," he said suddenly and awkwardly, having found nothing cleverer.

She looked at him sharply for a second and answered: "Why?"

He showed her his drawing of her. "It isn't finished, you see."

"You picked the wrong model," she said, smiling.

"No, I think the others did."

"It is true she is hard to do; there is an awful lot to dispose of."

Edward looked at her drawing, in which the model had been over-refined.

"I see you are given to improvements and to anemia," he said, and immediately feared he had lost her. He was elated to see her laugh.

"I'm so glad you are frank! Tomorrow you can help me be realistic. Au revoir."

She arrived the next day at half past nine. She wore, Edward observed, a dark blue velvet suit which made her look like a page from medieval stories. Her hat looked jaunty and yet soft, and when it was hung up in the hallway among the other tailored beige, brown and neutral colored ones, it looked unmodern, and it made him feel that just as the class had picked the wrong model she had picked the wrong century. But since he lived in this century and was fully able to appreciate her there was nothing wasted.

She smiled at him, but she was thinking of something else. This was the mystery he was intent on clearing. Where did her thoughts go when they were not on her drawing. Not to other centuries; she was carrying a book of Cocteau about. But she had a fearful way of looking high over the heads of everybody, and through walls.

Edward could think of nothing better than to criticize the quality of her chalk and pencils so that he might suggest where she should buy them. With sweet docility she met him there after class. He enjoyed seeing her shop, talk, move, even argue. She was real. She could even count her money quickly.

When they came out it was raining. Edward shivered as realistically as he could and said in an accent of profound distress: "How good a cup of coffee would taste now. Have you ever been to the Viking?"

His model looked at her watch. "I have plenty of time. Let's."

This rather startled him, although he had keenly hoped for it. She knew the Viking, then; she was accustomed to drinking coffee, not alone, and she even knew how much time it all required. Edward had forgotten they were in Montparnasse, two yards from the Grande Chaumiere.

She told him she knew he was the author of some very keen impressionistic sketches of night life, of market women, rag pickers, and policemen.

He told her all he fancied about her. And came back three times to his question, "So you have been here often?" with a sort of anxious curiosity.

"Yes, many times. Isn't that natural?"

"No," he said, rather gloomily.

"But why not? Why not? I'm alive, Edward Lunn, I'm modern. You have simply taken a painter's liberty and dated me rather far back. An 1830 face you said. That's possible. But not my mind." She leaned over, laughing, and touched his hand as if to emphasize her humanness. He looked so startled she withdrew it instantly.

"Don't tell me," she said, "that you are an idealizer of women, and that you see an aureole of poetry around my head!"

"The modern flippancy does not suit you at all," he said. "It's a pose."

"I'm sorry," said Chantal, "I teased you. You were dreaming. I did it to break the spell. I always do it to break the spell. I have become suspicious of dreaming. I did a lot of it myself once, and while I was doing it many agreeable things, real things, passed me by."

"I hate real things," said Edward, looking around rather bearishly at the rest of the people.

Chantal knew he had not understood.

They exchanged books and arguments while touring the Luxembourg Gardens under one umbrella. They discussed psychology over the cafe tables of the Boule Mich. They shared the love of painting while working side by side at the Grande Chaumiere. And while hunting down special books along the quays, they felt the excitement and the fever of mental communion.

Paris was newer to him than to Chantal who had been born in it. She had to wait around the corners, sometimes, with a little watchful smile, while he made his discoveries. They were very old discoveries. Chantal wanted sometimes to mock them. His surprise and his elation were so childlike. Then she realized he was discovering himself, and was silent, soft eyed, and patient. He had drawn things exactly as he had seen them and with such intuition that they suggested all the meaning there was in them to others. But what they suggested was beyond Edward's own knowledge and understanding. His little women had heavy eyes, and faces one could imagine any moment altered by a violent enjoyment of the senses; his men wore sardonic smiles, and all his people in the street the skepticism and mellowness of an old race. But it was all accuracy of drawing, and he himself had no key to the meaning of his work.

She took him to the Salon des Humoristes and they laughed together. She put many French books in his way. She saw that he was stirred to a new conception of fearless living. His mind grew bright and flexible. He saw that from her hands came a warm knowledge, but he still thought her a legendary apparition.

One morning they were all working intently when Chantal noticed that the model's body was trembling a little. After a minute she slipped down on the model stand, took her head in her hands and sobbed. Someone in the front row rushed up to her with her kimono and covered her. "Are you cold?" they asked her. She went on sobbing and mumbling. Chantal went up to her. The model was Russian and knew little French but she finally explained that she had not eaten for three days. Chantal asked her to be patient for a few minutes, and ran out to the cafe, and came back with a boy carrying coffee, Porto and a basket of brioches. The boy stared at the model. Chantal sent him away. The whole class was chattering and commenting, but only three persons stood near the model. Edward looked upset. She was sitting as Chantal had left her, with her knees under her, her kimono open at the front which she did not bother to close.

In general they all showed a callous indifference to the model during working hours. She was like a piece of furniture. Few of the students talked with her. Knowing her body so intimately seemed to eliminate her value as an individual. But here, crying, eating her brioche, and her face swollen, and her kimono hanging loose, she suddenly became someone to have a feeling about. Chantal pitied her. Edward did not talk, but looked troubled. One woman drew her kimono around her tightly, "You must not catch cold," she said. Then she turned away. One placid elderly man asked if she wanted him to take up a collection for her.

Suddenly Chantal noticed a change on Edward's face. His eyes were on the woman's body, still heaving a little. It was not the same look he had while he was drawing.

After a while they all went back to work. But Chantal could
not draw anymore. She had been shadowing the breasts, to bring
out their swelling and the angle at which they fell, a little sideways,
with their overripeness. But she could not see pure lines anymore.
It seemed to her that the breasts were still heaving and trembling.
Chantal could not understand why, when the model had taken her
face with her wet hands to whisper in her ear, she had wanted to
move away.

Edward stopped working too. "I'm through for this morning,"
he said, without looking at her.

As several of them walked out together they left some money
on the model stand, but they did not look at the model.

Edward came to Chantal's studio late one evening. He
appeared restless and tense, seemed unwilling to sit, as was his
habit, next to the books. He looked out of the window, into
darkness, and finally came to stand in front of Chantal and without
looking at her, he burst out: "I suppose you have guessed it, I am
obsessed by that woman."

"The model," said Chantal quietly, as if to herself. And she
looked far beyond him. He, thinking she sought to meet his eyes,
bowed his head. "Oh, but you can't possibly understand what she
means to me. She has taught me joys, joys such as I never
suspected the existence of. No other moments in my life seem
worth remembering, no, not even those when I did my best work,
and God knows I thought I had reached then the heights of
ecstasy. My feeling for you, that is entirely apart: it's religious.
Let me talk to you, Chantal. I need you."

"You can talk to me."

"Forgive me for talking about her, but here with you is the
only peace and coolness I know. The other is like a fever, which
wears me out, like bad fever, a horrible thirst. I need her so much,
want her so much. I go to her. We spend the day together in her
room, but when I go away I do not feel satisfied, and yet I have
been fearfully happy." He sat on the edge of a chair and breathed
deeply.

"It's queer, here I feel freer. It is the light atmosphere of
your intelligence, of your calm will. The other woman dominates
me and all my senses. I can't think. I can't work. I can only

enjoy her; I am only aware of her. In a way that powerful forget-fulness is sweet, terribly sweet. I can't give it up, I can't give it up."

"I know, I know." Her voice was very gentle, and she almost crooned the words.

"You couldn't know! You sense things, you understand, you never say the wrong word, you are healing, but you can't *know*. It's like an explosion of the whole world. Nothing else matters or means anything except that intoxication of the senses. And that woman, would you believe it, warned me against herself, the first day. She said: "Go away before I teach you joys that you will never get from the kind of women you admire. Go back to your dear wholesome comrades." She despised me as she said it. I stayed. It has been the devil trying not to be sentimental. She is so callous, and I did not want her to think me ridiculous. Do you know what I sent her yesterday instead of flowers? An electric radiator — she has been cold in her hotel room — a radiator!"

He was laughing. He stood up and walked around the room. Suddenly he noticed that Chantal had not laughed.

"Why do you think I can't understand? I have known all those feelings. *My* will has been dissolved. I have known that forgetfulness . . ."

"*You* Chantal, *you!* But your face, your extraordinarily pure face!"

"Never mind my face from now on," she said crisply.

He sat down and looked crushed.

"Aren't you glad," she said very softly, "since it is because of that I can understand you today?"

"Glad? Glad? But how can I be glad when I have lost my ideal of you?"

"Well, I am glad of *that,*" said Chantal, looking very soft and human, leaning over a little, waiting.

But he did not understand.

THE PEACOCK FEATHERS

There was a white house with enormous windows always
open and staring at the sea over the heads of the palm trees. She
had been born in a place like that.

The white path sprouted out of the heart of the house and
led downhill to the sea. It was edged with bristly cactus, long
fingered, writhing, thick and furry, unmoved by the sea breeze.
Over the ageless cactus the bamboo shoots trembled close together,
perpetually wind-shirred.

There was a lady in the white house who had collected birds
from all parts of the world, birds of changeful plumage, vitreous
cries and velvety manners who paced the thin alleys during the day
and were very still at night. Every night the sound of the sea
was covered by that of music.

That night the sea was almost asleep, and the birds and the
breeze were silent. A woman's fluted voice slid out into the
garden, down the path in a circle, trilling into space. The white
house was full of people who were gathered near the windows to
breathe an air which was bristling with the current of close-set
tropical stars.

The women sighed in their very tight silk dresses as the voice
of the singer brushed their breasts. The men were bent a little
forward with attentiveness.

The husband of the singer stood by the enormous open door,
one foot on the gravel of the path. He alone did not look at the

singer. Out of the darkness of the garden there came a peacock who waddled slowly into the long column of light, with his fan tail open.

He paced up to the open door thoughtfully. The husband looked at him; the peacock paced up towards the voice and listened. He never moved from there until the singing died down. Only when the clapping came, he closed his fan tail and went back into the darkness.

The next day the peacock was dead.

The lady of the house had the peacock's feathers brought to her and with a note she had them delivered to the singer.

The singer received them with a cry: "Oh, they bring bad luck, I know they do! Yet they are too beautiful to throw away. And besides," she said to her husband, "I think it was quite touching last night how that peacock listened to my singing."

And she wrote the lady a note of thanks.

The peacock feathers were placed in a flower vase, against the orange walls of her room.

Her husband did not notice them. He was trying not to notice anything about her now. Once he had loved her for her voice and had walked into a concert hall with the same still ensorcellment of the peacock. He had gone to the artist room where she was receiving profuse tribute from a crowd. He had asked her to come out with him alone to a quiet place where they might talk of music. During his travels he had unearthed some very old Italian songs which were quite unknown. She laughed and said: "But there's a big supper being given for me tonight by a group of friends. Why don't you join us?"

He had gone away with the same slow pace of the peacock when he had heard the applause. They met again in a place in Italy when she was singing and he had come up to her after the song and told her that he loved her.

Now they had been married many years and he never listened when she was singing for after each time there were many people around her and she loved all they said to her and believed them. She sang to them, and for them, for the things they said when they crowded around her and drank to her triumph.

That day, when the peacock feathers were only in the flower vase a few hours, he sat down and wrote her a farewell note and walked down into dark gardens and into silence.

She looked at the feathers and said: "They are the cause of my misfortune."

But she went on with her singing. In Egypt she met a young musician and she sang his compositions so that he would love her. He was at the beginning of his career. She did not let him work any longer but demanded all his time for herself, and he soon ceased composing, and merely followed her wherever her concert tours took her. She was tired of his adoration and began to sing the songs of other young composers. Then at a very big concert, in front of everybody, he killed himself while she was singing, and ruined her triumph.

It is the fault of the peacock feathers, she thought.

She would have thrown them away but for the face that a poet had said to her: "You can well afford to defy destiny because you are beautiful and talented." And so she dared the peacock feathers to do her harm.

She wrote her memoirs as she was sure she would be admired for them. She had known so many years of brilliant living and had always been surrounded by celebrities. In her memoirs she tried to make herself sensitive and tender-hearted. She wrote mincingly and studied her effects carefully. Yet when the memoirs were read they revealed calculatedness, and there were many people who satirized her.

As she had written them with a pen made out of one of the peacock feathers she thought: It is the fault of the peacock feathers.

Once in a Hindu home she was offered a long pipe. The smoking of it gave her marvellous dreams. She saw ships of sapphire sailing on seas of coral, and she at the prow singing. She felt herself raised on a light cloud of cotton into a sphere where her voice flowed like liquid light. Circles of strange personages listened to her with astonishment. Then she descended into dark caves where warmth and perfumes dissolved her and she was loved by resplendent men whose love had a thousand and one ways of penetrating her. But when she ceased smoking she was empty of all energy and looked haggard. Her voice altered too and she lost her power over her audience who once listened to her with the same rapt fixity of the peacock. In spite of that she could not stop smoking, because of the lulling effect on her and she said it is the fault of the peacock feathers.

Now her life was destroyed but she kept the feathers with more care than ever so as to be able to say to those who observed her ruin: It was the fault of the peacock feathers.

FAITHFULNESS

Aline was pleased that Alban should want to call on her that afternoon. She had seen him often striding about Montparnasse with books under his arms, never sitting at cafes, which was enough to brand him as a peculiar sort. As a matter of fact, it was because she had said one night at a studio party that the cafe was originally a meeting place, a center of conversation, a market for ideas, but that it had degenerated into a zoo, that Alban pounced into her group and never stopped talking to her the rest of the evening.

Aline teased him about the cafes. He told her he carried this attitude further:

"I frequent only the little white bakeries where nothing ever happens. The waitress stops mending her stockings by the side of the cash register to bring me a cup of milk which does not sit very steadily on the bread crumbs left by other people. The flowers in the little jars are faded. Nobody talks about the unconscious with fashionable consciousness. Children come in for their bread and chocolate. The whiteness of the bakery walls is like the whiteness of a sanatorium. There I recuperate from the inquisitiveness and the biological complications of the zoos."

"But are you as whitewashed mentally as all that?" asked Aline, "I do appreciate wholesomeness in food, but in people . . ." She made a wry face.

"Oh, no," said Alban, "because I am a playwright! But I could ask you the same question. What is the meaning of your early morning walks in the Luxembourg, when you smile at the children, the little dogs, the old men, the flowers?"

"It is difficult, isn't it, to find something original to do in Montparnasse, but I think you and I have."

When Alban came, even before he sat down, he confessed he had been afraid to come: "I'll tell you frankly, when you talked about the zoo, I wondered if you meant it! Some people say that only because they like to transport the whole show at home. You never see them alone. On the sacred and clearly printed day you are thrust into a roomful of people you had not asked for. They call it having a salon. Or perhaps, perhaps I came the wrong day?"

"No, this is what I like. But you must admit some people must be mixed with others to be endured."

"I never endure. I board a train, a ship, an airplane."

"But you might open your door wilfully to the wrong person. Don't you ever make mistakes? How do you choose your friends?"

"I let them talk," said Alban.

"You did not let me put in one word the other night!"

"Oh, that was a special occasion. You are such a good listener! It was such a marvellous thing to find at Henri's party that I could not resist the joy of testing it. It's funny how you listen. You never say a word, but just by a mere twinkle of the eyelid, a change in the color and shadows of your eyes, the merest curve in the corner of your mouth, you fill the silence with the keenest appreciation, and one feels like going on, going on. You should be the wife of a writer."

"But I don't listen all the time," said Aline.

It was Alban who did not listen so well, but as she talked, he analyzed her face with an intense, puzzled frown.

"You have very unusual eyes," he said, without any effort at coherence. "Veiled and tragically discontented."

"I make allowances for your playwright's imagination, but I can't see why they should appear that way at all," she said, getting up and walking to the window. "It's raining," she added gravely.

"I see you are upset by my remark. I'm sorry. It is not very European to burst out with one's private opinion the first day. I came to Europe to learn detours and subtlety. Haven't learned much of it, have I? Are you angry?"

Aline was closing the curtains, lighting the candles, and opening a new box of cigarettes.

"Lovely atmosphere here," he said. "But it isn't all *you*. You make concessions to your husband. Here are the pipes, the Economic Magazine, the office armchair, and a photograph of the President of the Company. I like to imagine something else for you, a sort of Orientalism, divans, and fresh fruit on plates inlaid with coral and turquoise."

"We can't have fresh fruit in the house; my husband is on a diet; it has to be cooked." And then: "I think you are hateful."

"Don't force me into a bromide about the painfulness of truth."

"What truth?"

"That you are mentally unaccompanied. Furthermore, do you know what I predict? That you are going to settle down to a dead felicity and domesticity, absolutely incurable, because women fear that kind of loneliness more than domesticity. Already I noticed the other evening when your husband came into our group that your mind did not leap and shine anymore. You waited for his conjugal approval!"

"What do you think he would have thought if I had gone on mixing bakeries and the unconscious? Anyway, you are right. I have my peaceful days already, when I am tired, or when the rain depresses me, so it won't take me long to become what you predict I will become."

"You aren't taking me a bit seriously," said Alban, "and yet you are so unhappy."

"Do you know a remedy?"

"Friends," said Alban. "I always give that solution in my plays."

"Friends in the Montparnasse way?" said Aline mockingly.

"Next time I'll bring you the play in which I settled the problem definitely. It will convince you."

When he was gone Aline began to think it would be a pity if she had nothing to be consoled for. Alban, with his fanciful manners, must be interesting in such crises. He had a fertile and varied mind, and he was not a genius whose face and figure one had to make allowance for.

So she went quietly about the house, pleasantly accumulating and calculating her misfortune. It was true she was often condemned to talk to herself, that when she read Sherman her stories he either grunted or said: "That's nice." It was true that very often when she was overjoyed by a long afternoon of sizzling good writing, he often dissolved her exhilaration by dragging her to a tennis match.

There was no doubt that Alban had imagination, an energetic one, and she had always been fascinated by story tellers.

For the first time in several years, that evening, she looked at her husband very attentively and with detachment.

Sherman always wore rather heavy suits and looked very dependable. His eyes contained authority, a quiet wisdom, nothing stormy or spectacular. He talked little, and listened with a kind of rumination which, if Aline inquired further, sometimes turned out to be a mere mask to profound calculations on stocks. He knew how to read the substantial philosophers. He had a mind that perceived wisdom, sitting down, as other people gather the phases of temperature through a window and a barometer. He was convinced beforehand by a natural respect for knowledge about all those ready-made phrases taught by long dead poets. He had done dutifully all the lyrical things prescribed by them, and done them systematically.

But Aline could not remain forever in that rarified atmosphere, satisfied with the mere joy of fitting theories together. She had to come down to some warm extension of such words and to some mad test of their true meaning.

He was shaving. They were going out to Bellow's studio for a musical evening.

"Have you ever thought," she asked, "how one could be influenced by one's own writing?" She had a strong desire to talk about Alban's plays.

"No," said Sherman, "I never did." He was intensely pre-occupied with a certain area under his chin. His hand never wavered. She waited until he was finished to give him time to form an opinion. But he was entirely dressed and had not spoken yet, so she asked him, at the end, what he thought.

"About what? Oh, that influence business . . . Er . . . well . . . nothing."

"You don't think it would be possible?"

"I don't know. But listen here, what is this you are carrying on, an inspection?"

"No," said Aline. "An autopsy."

Bellows had mixed a lot of discordant personalities that night in his apartment and hoped to appease them with music. He played for them with tremendous fervor, talked with the same concentration, and took no notice whatever of the traps set him by the young ironists. He had an enormous head set on a small, wasted body, long fingers which clutched the notes with a knotty strength. He compositions, all in minor keys, suggested a diabolical unreality.

There was a singer there. There is usually a singer about pianists and violinists, like secretaries about bankers, and things happen between them that newspapers are glad to hear about.

This one was a Jewess with a tragic face and beautiful arms. But as soon as she spoke her face proved to be an accident and there remained only the arms which were undeniably enough to make up for her talk. Bellows was particularly gentle about her talk. He did not listen to it. He looked at her arms, and Aline was sure he felt them around his neck. To her he offered as a tribute the sacrifice of his Germanic ideas on music, and did not insist when she praised the Italians.

At first she was a little worried about Aline. Aline had worn a subtle, insidious dress, revealing and concealing the figure at the same time, oriental in essence, complex in its embroidery, utterly unintelligible to Bellows, but the singer understood it, and objected to it.

But when she had sat nobly, with all the ripeness of her forty years, nobly and comfortably, with her round smooth arms over the red arms of the chair, she realized, as Aline realized, that Aline could not fill her chair nor any Germanic ideal of beauty. And then she set out for a calm enjoyment of the evening, using her arms to describe the flow of Verdi's music, and to bring up continuously around her a slippery coat with brown fur.

Aline's husband grew sleepy, and they went home early.

Bellows came to see her without his singer. Aline really wanted to ask him why. She said very impulsively: "I'm sorry, my husband is not home," and waited for him to go. He looked so much like the kind of man such things would frighten away. But he was even more tactless and said: "I did not expect to see him."

"Well, well, sit down, Mr. Bellows." (And Aline had thought he admired Wagnerian proportions exclusively!). She led him to the piano. He played only what he loved for her; and then he made musical portraits of the singer mocking her love of Italian street melodies, lingering on the notes sentimentally.

"But you like her," said Aline.

"That doesn't prevent me from knowing that she should still be singing over her orange cart, where I found her. Now I'll make you a portrait of my concierge." Note by note, in minor keys, the dragon came up the stairs. The music grew solemn and awecome, and then demoniac. The concierge's gruesome voice broke into a vindictive outburst. Bellows answered with ironic sweetness, and banged his door. She labored down the stairs with a clatter of wooden shoes. Aline, leaning over the piano, on her elbows, laughed.

"And now your husband," said Bellows. He played Bach. He was scholarly, he was precise, he was very superb and classical. Bellows exaggerated Bach's measure. Before Aline could say anything, he was making a quizzical portrait of Henri, the sculptor, and a highly colored description of Alban. Alban required all the keyboard, and reached an almost orchestral importance.

"Now me." He was grotesque, he was unsteady, and yet the ascent of a tormented melody finally reached one note of triumph.

"Have you understood that," he asked, almost furtively.

"You reached serenity by the power of the mind, by overlooking details," said Aline.

"And you," he said, "will never reach it."

"Do I look troubled?" said Aline.

Bellows played a fantastic strain. In the middle of it he stopped with a violent dissonance. Aline made a wry face.

"That is you and your husband," said Bellows.

"You are quite mistaken."

"I may be a clumsy old brute, but it seems to me you don't love him." He had moved his chair close, and was tapping her fingers, tapping them lingeringly, and shaking his big head compassionately.

"You're all wrong there, Mr. Bellows."

"I admire your courage, you dear, lovely, spirited young thing. You don't want to say anything, and yet those things are much easier to face if you can talk about them." He pressed her hand tenderly, significantly, tentatively.

"Well," she thought, when he was gone, "That's the limit." And could not wait for her husband to come home. She watched for him at the window; she rushed to meet him in the hallway, her big young husband. "If you only knew what happened to me!"

He cautiously closed the door.

"Think of it," she blurted out, her face aflame with indignation. "Imagine, imagine, old Bellows telling me I didn't love you, you my darling! Thinking I was bravely hiding my unhappiness, tapping my hands with his hairy ones to console me. Can you imagine such nerve, such nerve! Whoever told *him* I needed consoling!"

He laughed at her anger. Her voice was swelling and she could not speak fast enough. He leaned over suddenly and kissed her, still heaving inwardly: "You dear, faithful, honest little wife," he said.

A SPOILED PARTY

The Stellams' apartment was filled with noise and people. The orchestra played continuously and frantically. The dancers were laughing. Groups of shining women and trim glossy men were still arriving.

Mrs. Stellam herself was sheathed in a crystal beaded costume, showing all of her softly moulded shoulders and back. She teased the men with a red feather fan which she waved constantly like an exotic plant. Everywhere she stood there formed a cloud of perfume.

She was quite conscious of being beautiful, of being appreciated, and of having a reputation for imagination. She herself knew how much she studied her fantasies, and how well prepared her impulses were. Like this party, for instance. She had had the idea of dividing the room up into little tables for two or four people as in a cabaret. The orchestra was in Cossack costume.

'This will be a successful party,' said Mrs. Stellam to herself. 'Almost like a fete in a Russian palace. How well my arched doorways look, and the odd lanterns, and how the coral colored walls set off every one and seem to act on their mood for they are all so brilliant and excited.'

Quite unexpectedly Mrs. Stellam found herself facing a woman she did not know. The woman was beautifully costumed in emerald green, watery silk. She had very long, very glossy turquoise-colored eyes and sienna hair which stood out around her head airily.

Mrs. Stellam greeted her politely and thought she must be someone's new wife and that the husband must be somewhere else and had forgotten about introductions. The stranger answered the greeting quietly with a nod and a smile, but did not mention her name. Mrs. Stellam waited to see who she would turn and speak to.

The stranger walked slowly across the room, not bowing to anyone in particular, but all who saw her bowed vaguely to her.

'I never invited her,' thought the hostess irritably, 'yet I cannot throw her out. Someone must have brought her. It must be a trick of Henley's. He is always doing that sort of thing. He will have to come and dance with her, and then I will be sure.'

But it was becoming quite plain that the stranger did not know anyone. The dancing began again. Her face was constantly smiling as she had smiled at the hostess, with very open, rather staring eyes. Her smile was slightly mocking but her eyes were very serious and intense.

One man spoke to her over his glass of champagne, vaguely, as men speak to a woman they have been following in the street: "We have met before?"

She looked fixedly at him, and as he looked the smile seemed to broaden to fantastic amusement. But when he looked at the eyes they were almost intolerably serious. He was thoroughly annoyed and walked away.

Another man came tripping over and with a familiar gesture took her out to dance. She was very flexible and light but she did not talk. The man flattered her. She merely looked on at him, almost with contempt, he thought, yet at the same time her eyes shone so very pleasingly and simply. He grew hot and uncomfortable and began to dance awkwardly.

The party grew even noisier. Balloons were flung in the air and exploded. Confetti was thrown into eyes and mouths. Some of the men imitated animal grunts and whinings and bellowings; others fed themselves nervously on salted almonds to create more thirst for champagne. Face powder showed clearly on the men's lapels, and there were patterns of big moist hands on the frail silks of the women's dresses. Some crystal beads had been scattered on the floor, and someone had dropped an artificial carnation.

But around the stranger the voices were pitched lower and there was no laughter.

A woman asked the hostess who the stranger was. "That emerald dress certainly comes from a Grande Maison," she said. Mrs. Stellam grew more and more irritable. She could not ask the stranger to leave; by her manners and dress she seemed to belong there. The butlers were intimidated and served her assiduously, and the butlers had an instinct about such things.

From far away her smile seemed so harmless and pleasing. Many men would cross the room, full of confidence and gaity, to take her out to dance, and it was only when they stood very near her that they would find the smile intolerable. Whenever she passed, a loud laugh would suddenly die, and women's small, fretty, or coquettish gestures become awkward. Certain talks were cut short and never taken up again, certain couples would look uncomfortable together and draw apart and remain so.

The jazz increased in intensity, whipping the nerves to jerks and rhythms, knocking on the heart. The stranger did not touch the drinks but her face became more and more vivid, and her smile was so brilliant no other woman dared to smile. People were growing uneasy. The jazz kept on and the bodies jerked but the faces became dark and conscious.

Certainly the party was dying down, and it was only one o'clock. Mrs. Stellam was desperate. The stranger sat there, silent and unconcerned, as on a desert island.

'She must go now,' thought Mrs. Stellam. 'I will go up and speak to her.'

They stood now and faced each other. Mrs. Stellam darted her eyes coldly into the eyes of the stranger.

Then she saw in them that the stranger knew her as no one else had ever known her, knew the woman nobody knew. There was no doubt about it. Her clear eyes, very intense, serious eyes had seen . . . had seen Mrs. Stellam's comedy of clothes, and home, and friendship, and marriage, all the things on which she had merely used her power, her power to hold, to alter, to destroy. All her activities had been destined to that sole end, to dominate, to hurt, for the sake of that exultant feeling of infinite power. In the stranger's eyes she saw all that, herself entire and real, and with her she looked fearlessly, directly, silently. All the while there was no talk to cover up the discovery, no talk such as many times Mrs. Stellam had taken refuge in when she had been on the point of self-discovery. It seemed to Mrs. Stellam as she faced the stranger's broad smile and admitted the truth of all she had seen, that the smile grew less sharp at the edges, just slightly less sharp, almost soft.

Suddenly Mrs. Stellam turned away from her and rushed to the jazz band and asked them to play their loudest jazz.

But everybody began to leave. There was a bustle of fur coats and hats and umbrellas and canes, and soft emanations of perfume slipping out of unfolded coats.

Goodbye, goodbye! There was a lot of handkissing and thanks for the party.

The stranger was wrapped in grey furs; the tips of the fur were silvered and glowed and bristled. She too was on her way out.

"Oh, I am sorry, I am sorry you have to go," said Mrs. Stellam.

She looked into the stranger's eyes. It was a tremendous relief to look into her eyes, a relief from complications and evasions. "Will I ever see you again?"

The stranger smiled but shook her head. "I come only once."

A SLIPPERY FLOOR

Anita gave hurried orders to the maid. She packed her castanets and her ballet slippers. She waxed her eyelashes, blued her eyelids, and powdered more than usual, because it was the day set for rehearsing.

When she first went down the dark stairway leading to Alamilla's studio, she still felt quiet and mousy. There was nothing theatrical about her black hat and coat. But when she opened the door and heard the sudden sharp sound of Alamilla's castanets rolling like a small drum, and when he himself came forward to greet her with: "Here you are, little gypsy!" then she felt like another woman.

Her Spanish dress hung all aflutter on the first nail to the right in the dressing room. Along the other nails hung ballet dresses, two Spanish dresses, an old sweater, an old towel, and there were ballet slippers on the chairs, on the shelves, on the washstand, everywhere, until they reached the overflowing scrap basket at the end of their ephemeral career.

When she had her dress on she looked at the mirror to put her earrings on, and the carnation. On the shelf before the mirror was an old newspaper in which she read every day that a passion crime had been committed Thursday on the Rue Notre Dame. She never got further than the description of the lover, who had brown eyes, a grey suit, and a jealous disposition. She never knew what the lady who had been the cause of the crime looked like. She could have read the end of the story if she had not always been interrupted by the women who rehearsed before her. Here came one of them, perspiring, glowing, a big healthy woman with a brown skin, and all the convincing toughness required by music hall life. But her hair did not stick down as well as Anita's, and Anita had been hesitating for two weeks at giving away her secret. Today in a fit of sublime generosity she told her: "Use Gomina." The dancer gave her an unexpectedly natural smile and answered: "I'll tell you where you can get your shoes soled with rubber so you won't slip when you dance."

Alamilla immediately began to call her. He did not like them to talk. He was afraid that like two really tempermental Spanish dancers they would soon begin to pull each other's combs out. But the woman whose hair did not stick down was from Montmartre, and Anita was only half Spanish.

"Next time you borrow my petticoat," said Anita before leaving, "you'd better sew up the tear so I won't know it!"

That made up for the 'Gomina'.

It was dark when she came out. The Place Clichy was illuminated with colored lights, with the yellow lights of the little and big cafes, with the white lights of the Fair. The music of the merry-go-rounds was so off tune that it sounded like melodies of an absolutely unknown country. And Anita did not care to recognize them as the ones she heard in other parts of Paris. She felt that she was really off on a strange voyage, among thin-shouldered people with smouldering eyes, whose unsteady hands were constantly lighting cheap cigarettes, whose hoarse voices were always calling for drinks. She would be tossed up to some corner table of a cafe, tossed up like driftwood by that crowd which moved like a sea, by the heavings and fermentations of Parisian life.

The Place Clichy and its surroundings remained the goal of all her trips. It seemed to her that the very bus which took her to the theatrical section was full of special people. They got off at the Casino and the Apollo. While the bus stopped there she sat in the glare of the electric signs, and lived, for a moment, a little of her dreams, cheap dreams of heavy makeup, dazzling spotlights, a dark audience applauding her, and behind the stage vivid people to live with. In the electric stars, sun-bursts, and diamond serpents of the

Casino, she saw the symbols of a fantastic destiny. She wanted a fantastic destiny instead of a wise one, brilliance instead of harmony, endless voyages, the perpetually shifting ground of stage life, rather than security.

When she walked alone her eyes naturally sought the lights, the crude and startling ones of the little shops, the dancing and skipping ones around the advertisements, the red arrows which burned down the subway stairs, those which flashed the "Revue de Paris" into the sky, and eclipsed the stars. All in black, with her valise, her castanets, and an Andalusian rhythm in her head, she followed the lights.

A young man stopped her, a young man with a face burnt up with swift living, a handsome face lined by old emotions, with eyes that had seen everything. He smiled a smile quite certain of its charm: "Tu es trop jolis pour te promener seule." She looked into that face which had seen everything. She caught a spark of mockery at the very bottom of his eyes. The surface of them shone back at the lights, like glass. Underneath they were dim, as if burnt up. She darted away from him. That time she was a little late for the rehearsal. When she came out the evening mist had dimmed the lights, a mist which did not come down from the skies but which rose like the breath of the earth through the hard pavement.

Anita's first engagement was in a small ballet, in a small theatre.

Two men sat in the Director's office the day she came to sign her contract.

"Your partners," said the Director, and to them: "The Spanish dancer Mr. Boris, is a Russian who has been in Spain many years training for Spanish dancing. Mr. Lasa is a South American who will take the part of the gypsy. You'd better start at once — we haven't much time. You can begin the composition of the dances. The pianist is waiting for you. Tomorrow you will see the costumer."

They all discreetly looked each other over. Boris came and stood next to Anita. Lasa said: "You are just the right size for each other."

Anita observed that Boris was not over-affected by his good looks.

They began the dance and the mimicry. Anita wore an oldish gypsy dress, with a flaring red petticoat. She danced around Boris in a circle of undulations, to bewitch him. It was absolutely necessary that she should bewitch him in the ballet. Lasa sat smoking and watching them, waiting his turn. Boris simulated passion with a perfect technique.

"Don't forget to be careful of my comb," said Anita.

"I won't be careful of anything when I abduct you," said Lasa. "I'm a primitive gypsy."

The stage was small. Chairs had been placed where in future there would be a Palace wall, trees, and a fountain.

The electrician was interested, and let his work wait while he watched from his ladder. But the cleaner was an old-timer and she want on raising dust while they worked. The actors of the serious play which was to precede the ballet, began to arrive and to claim the stage.

"How long have you been in the business?" asked Lasa.

"One day."

"And you didn't trip! You show promise."

"We'll adopt you," said Boris.

"Do you know how to make up?"

"Do you know how to bow?"

"How to escape being knocked on the head when the curtain comes down?"

"How to warm up alone in a frozen crowd?"

"Know anything about lights?"

"I'm not afraid of anything," said Anita, "except of tearing my petticoat."

"If you have money, we'll invite you to have a drink with us when you're dressed," said Lasa.

It was a very small cafe. The Spring had not entered it yet. They had forgotten the stove outside, with ashes in it. The little stove usually kept burning on cold days so people could sit outside even in winter. Boris and Lasa rested their feet on it while they talked.

"What do you expect of the stage? What do you know about stage life?" Boris asked her. "Are you a dream-swallower?"

She remembered her wild dreams of brilliant living, and that worldly-wise look in the young man's eyes which she had both liked and hated, but she could not tell tham about that.

"It's true I have no experience," she admitted. "But I do know a lot about stage life, and I'm no dream-swallower."

"How do you know?" asked Lasa.

"Oh, I've read, I've read enormously," said Anita. And she began a vast, inclusive gesture, which she finished a little more vaguely as she realized that she did not remember the names of the books she had read. "Colette, for example . . . many others . . . ," she finished lamely.

Boris' eyes were laughing. Lasa took a drink and was silent.

What troubled her these days was that her dressing room had no door, just a shrunken curtain of cretonne. While she dressed and undressed people would burst in with messages, or to borrow her cold cream, or her towel. After the rehearsal one day she rushed out in her kimono, still breathless from the dance, to see the manager, and ran into Boris who asked her what was the matter.

"There is no door to my dressing room."

"But there is never a door to a dressing room in little theatres like this."

"I will certainly catch cold," said Anita.

In her dressing room she thought: "Well, I had wished for stage life, and I have got not only agreeable partners, amusing rehearsals, exciting spotlights, plenty of variety, but a room without a door. I had imagined everything but that: coming in and out in my kimono, receiving visitors while adding the very last touches to my dressing, but not dressing and undressing behind a shrunk curtain, before the electricians." That had not entered into her calculations at all. She had fully intended to be a good sport, very natural and very easy-going — but with a few aristocratic reservations.

She began testing out systems: putting a chair before the curtain so people would bump into it before they came in and that would give her time to put her kimono on. But a messenger passed and being in too much of hurry to come in he just stuck his head in at the corner without warning, and she had just time enough to delve into the shrunk curtain, incidentally hitting someone who was passing, jumping back, ghost-like, still wrapped in it, and reaching out for her kimono rather late.

"This is getting serious," she thought. She also tried to dress within her kimono, turning her back to the entrance. But she could be seen in the mirror. She tacked papers on the mirror. Boris saw it and asked her what was wrong. "The mirror is bluish," she said. "It depresses me to see myself in it."

"You can have my dressing room, it is better," said Boris.

It was at the end of the hall. Anita went to look at it. It did not even have a curtain.

That afternoon she was dressing fitfully within her kimono, entangled in the sleeves, when the carpenter appeared.

"Madame, will it bother you if I put the door on now? It won't take long. I only have to slip it on the hinges."

"So there were doors!" said Anita.

"But the old ones were breaking down."

She rushed out to find Boris. "What did you mean about the doors?"

"I just wanted to show you, my dear, that books don't teach everything."

"I hope then I can depend on *you*," said Anita with a look that was not complimentary.

The little table at the cafe, the three drinks, became a rite. Boris and Lasa told Anita they wanted to see her sober up. They talked to dissipate the vapors or some imaginary intoxication. But she gave no signs of defeat. She had fully expected monotony, routine, hard work, conflicts of vanity, squabbles. She showed no disappointment when Lasa revealed to her that her name would not shine in electric letters, and on the posters it would be in very small letters because the actors in the "serious" play were of more importance.

They also teased her about the fact that she had not lost her head and heart yet.

"The stage life does not *get* you as it should," said Lasa.

"What is it supposed to do to me?"

"Oh, you go into it heart and soul, you tumble in, you show

some excess of temperment, you fall in love . . . I have made love to you and you just smile."

"The same with me," said Lasa.

"But I just have not fallen in love," said Anita.

"Must you wait for that to play around a bit? I should think you couldn't help yourself."

"Oh, but that's my hobby," said Anita, "I believe I *can* help myself."

"And you've succeeded?"

"So far."

"A queer hobby! How did that idea come to you?"

Anita hesitated.

"Are we asking indiscreet questions? You know how fond we are of you."

"I know you are. I don't mind answering. I got the idea from my Father. I had a Mother I have never known who never denied herself any whim, however much it hurt others. She left home on account of one of them. I just got it into my head I would be as unlike my Mother as possible."

"But why then, of all things, did you choose to be a dancer? Of all the difficult propositions . . .!"

"I think I almost did it on purpose. From all I heard I gathered it would be the most difficult career in which to practice such a life. Besides, my Mother is an actress — her profession was always her excuse. I like having almost the same profession, and yet manage not to lose my head until I fall really in love. Are you amused?"

"We meet all kinds in our life," said Boris. "I wish you luck."

The opening night. In the small dressing room the big full skirted Spanish dress scarcely fits. Anita's eyes look twice their normal size after the black pencilling, the blue-green paste on the eyelids, and the waxed eyelashes. In the mirror she sees that her face is radiant, that the lace mantilla hangs well, that the three big carnations are firmly pinned. She wets the soles of her shoes. While she is dressing, Sanette comes to see if she has made up well. He inspects her face and says: "That's all right — but don't forget the red spots on the inner corners of the eyes."

From one dressing room to another, over the partitions, she hears a rush of talk, of exclamations and swearing. Boris' very tight vest has split a little. "It won't show under the cape," shouts Lasa consolingly. But Boris is upset. Lasa calls out that he has finished his brilliantine — has Boris any to lend him? Boris shouts back: "But you're a gypsy, you must not use brilliantine."

"En scene pour le premier acte!"

The serious play has begun.

Anita's hands are so cold she wonders if she will be able to play her castanets — they sound better when her hands are warm. She hears the other actors rushing out of their dressing rooms. She tries to lengthen her eyebrows, but her hand is not very steady. She adds a little Gomina to the black curls on her cheeks. Finally she comes out in the hall, and finds Boris ready, and trying to hurry Lasa. But there is plenty of time. The serious play has begun late, and it lasts an hour and a half. It is cold and drafty. There is a big invigorating bustle; orders and counter orders about lights, and the curtain, and the curtain again. The audience is heard laughing, and a little later they clap, spontaneously. The electricians are perched up on ladders at the left. There are rolled up rugs and furniture from other settings pushed into corners. There is nowhere to sit and many things to trip over. There are nervous scenes, delays, and a few mistakes. But some one always says reassuringly: "That's all right — the audience won't notice it." Anita wonders what else it will overlook.

Now for the ballet. Lasa smooths down one of Anita's ruffles. The white and orange lights are turned on.

Anita and Boris dance together. The very sight of the orange and black costume, and Boris' richly embroidered cape has brought a little "oh" of pleasure from the crowd. The dance is lively and colorful. Anita feels that she is carried away by an enormous, fantastic desire to dance beautifully to all that vast, still, dark expectancy before her. A new self takes hold of her, a self with double energy and double enthusiasm. A new woman, daring and assured, is released. Boris responds and dances with equal vigor and brilliance. The applause almost startles her. The ballet should be going on, but the public wants that dance again. From the darkness mounts a rush of enthusiasm. It makes her feel sure footed, light, expressive. She has to repeat her solo dance at the end. The curtain falls. She is very hot and very breathless. She has to come out and bow several times. When the curtain comes down for the last time she finds herself surrounded by strangers who bar the way to her dressing room, and praise her, and shake her hand. Someone gives her a shawl, and she wraps herself closely in it. Boris who stands beside her, receiving his share of compliments, whispers: "Try and answer one word, anyway." She is still a little blinded by the spotlight. She says: "Thank you, thank you," and tries to get into her dressing room. Boris shouts out to her: "Get dressed up for the supper: we're celebrating!"

It was a large table at the "Lion Amoureux". There were the managers, actors, a few critics, and a man who was talking of presenting the ballet in a bigger theatre. Anita sat between Boris and Lasa, and found on her plate a scrap book for the newspaper clippings. She was still very hot and a bit dazed. The waiters served her plentifully and smiled knowingly. She was draped in a white Spanish shawl. The jazz was so loud that there was little talk but much eye-signalling and laughter. She was taken out to dance by men who seemed to know little about Spanish dancing but a great deal as to the quality of eyes and ankles and waist she had displayed. She was asked to tea, to after-theatre suppers, to dance at a cabaret after the ballet. She was so tired she said "yes" to everything, hoping to untangle it all afterwards.

After that most nights began to resemble each other; there was always the tension, the climax, and a kind of collapse; half-hearted suppers after the show, newspaper criticism and praise, offers of small engagements, photographers, and reproductions of the photographs which never resembled her, and fervent letters from clerks and office boys.

The stir and bustle she grew as accustomed to as to calm. She dressed more quietly, answered more shortly, was less surprised, and had even a few suggestions to make to Lasa and Boris, the old veterans, who exhibited her as a dancer made while you wait, almost in forty eight hours.

The ballet changed theatres. It played successfully for four months. The Spring came and the foreigners began to arrive in Paris, but though the audience changed it was always responsive to the vivid story, the dramatic ending, and the colorful dancing.

Anita was beginning to think she was on her way to an interesting stage career.

One night after the show was over, and Anita had refused to have supper out because she was tired, a woman asked to be allowed in the dressing room (a larger dressing room now, full of mirrors).

"You don't recognize me, of course. I knew you wouldn't. You were only four when I left your Father."

Anita saw a woman twenty years or so older than herself, who resembled her astonishingly. This was the woman who had made her Father unhappy — that is all she knew. She had never thought of her, never asked for her, never wanted to know her. All she did know was that she had become an actress under a different name.

"Your Father never talked about me?"

"No," said Anita.

"It's natural you should have no particular feeling about me — you were such a baby. At that time I certainly never imagined you would take up such a career."

"Why does my career interest you?"

"It's a bond between us, isn't it? When I heard of your Father's death seven years ago I was undecided whether or not to let myself be known to you. I thought you might be a prim young girl, quite like him, severe even, interested only in books. Then I found out you turned out to be a dancer! What a tremendous joy that gave me. I thought you were *his* daughter, and I realize now you are *mine!*"

"But now I am used to being alone, to being nobody's daughter," said Anita, "I don't see that it makes much difference."

"Aren't you glad to see me?"

"I really don't know you, do I? How can I say?"

The woman laughed. "My, but you are modern! And I think I like it. I think we could understand each other wonderfully. We have had the same life, we have the same interests. Do you know what my stage name is? Vivien Foraine. Does that mean anything to you?"

"Yes," said Anita with pleasure. "I have heard people whose opinion is worth something say you were a fine actress."

"And I really think you are a splendid dancer. And very original."

"You have seen me?"

"Several times. You see, I wanted to know if I would like you before I introduced myself!"

"Thank you," said Anita.

"I am sorry you cannot say the same."

"You must give me time," said Anita gently.

"May I kiss you?"

The woman seemed quite a stranger. Perhaps her having made Anita's Father unhappy had created that strangeness, against any instinctive love. But Anita liked her presence, her voice, her manner, her brilliance. She could see in the mirror how keen the resemblance was, and the twenty years made little difference. Vivien was slender, beautifully dressed, made up, in the way of stage people, only very finely and carefully so. And for the first time Anita began to feel the pleasure of having someone related to you close to you. She had been quite alone now for seven years, all the while she had studied dancing.

"You have not had supper? Won't you come with me? Home?"

Home. That was an invitation which stirred Anita's curiosity. The woman seemed like a new friend, a friend in an easy going, unquestioning fashion, such as one picked up casually in her kind of life. Here today, gone tomorrow, on a tour perhaps. Her Mother was that to her, a friend, who might be gone tomorrow.

She did not realize that when she accepted to have supper with her, she accepted a home, from that night on.

After the meal, her Mother went on talking smoothly and continuously, offering her meanwhile, the guest room, a lacy negligee, jade green slippers.

"You look surprised. Why should you be? Our life is like that. Consider this part of your stage life: a sudden engagement. They do fall like that from a clear sky, don't they? An engagement to live with your Mother. (Look at my room. Do you care for changeable taffeta?) You can't imagine how much I had feared that you should resemble your Father, and be difficult and intolerant. It gave me much pleasure to see you dancing there, with such enthusiasm, such warmth and vigor, and to realize you might understand my life and my temperament better than he ever did. You will have to meet Norman. Norman is the one man I always come back to, whatever I do. He's a dear. (Here is the bathroom. What kind of bath salts do you like?) And you, my dear little Anita, have you no Norman waiting somewhere, wondering where you are tonight?"

"Not yet," said Anita, beginning to feel the strangeness and the loss of her independence. Yet it all looked so harmless, just very attractive, very pleasing to the eyes, and her Mother's sharp, light remarks were made in a wonderfully smooth voice, a voice that was very affecting, with deep rich low notes, as if she could be very warm and affectionate and comforting. Though just now she seemed to have her mind on perfume, on bedroom slippers, on the hour at which Anita might want her breakfast. "Like a week-end guest," thought Anita. But she was so tired she thought little about it. And the next day it seemed like a very old habit. She had only to advise the people about her hotel room, and to move. Both rehearsals were at about the same hours. They only met at lunch, and after the two shows.

Vivien took a great interest in Anita's costumes. To Vivien dressing was almost a religion, a ritual. On rainy days when everybody wore mousy or moth-eaten clothes she came out in a shining and vivid raincoat. She dressed in defiance of the elements rather than in submission to them. Anita could see that her dressing was almost a provocation to calmer inhabitants; things were bound to happen to Vivien, different things than happened to most women, she was always so dressed for it, for the unexpected, the adventurous. Her dressing roused in people an uneasiness similar to the feeling they had when looking over trip literature and pamphlets, a kind of wanderlust, a desire to flee from the familiar and the conventional. Whatever the stage possessed that enslaved the imagination Vivien had applied to her daily life. Between her setting and her costume, and the homes of other women and their costume lay a pit as wide as the orchestra pit in the theatre, and spotlights such as she directed on herself found her audaciously keyed up, as they found the professional actress.

Anita felt she had found a very interesting friend.

Anita had been told by Vivien she would not meet Norman for a week or so because he was away on a trip.

But on her way out to rehearsal one afternoon, when Vivien had already gone out, Anita met Norman at the door with his valise.

"Vivien wrote me about you," he said. "So you're Anita!"

"I am glad to meet you."

"Glad to meet you informally," said Norman. "Your Mother would have said: 'Norman Allard,' instead of 'my lover' — she is so refined."

"And she would have said: 'here is my little daughter', and I could not bear it."

"Vivien did not know you were arriving at this time," said Anita.

"I wanted to surprise her."

"She is having her hair waved."

"Oh, no," said Norman. "She is dancing at the Jardin Bleu. I know her." He said the words bitterly. "Does she tell you stories like that: she is having her hair waved! But then of course, she would. She is not sure you are absolutely like her, she wrote me. I see what she means."

"Don't you think we are alike?"

"In face, yes, in expression astonishingly different."

"I wonder what the difference is," said Anita.

"You will know soon," said Norman with a gesture of weariness. He had come in, meanwhile. He asked: "Must you go immediately?"

He looked very tired, very worried and tense. Anita felt sorry for him.

"No, I have twenty minutes or so."

"Then sit down here and talk to me. Did your Mother tell you why I went away?"

"No."

"Because I was so miserable, so tormented by her. It seems strange that I should talk to you about her when I hardly know you!"

"It is better that you should. I may be able to help you."

"She will probably convert you to her ideas. She is like that — so persuasive. Have you noticed what a lovely voice she has?"

"Yes, she has, but not all the time."

"Oh, you have noticed that, have you? Yet you love her!"

"I don't know if I do, yet," said Anita.

He looked almost amused. "You are different," he murmured. "Do you always say what you think, like that?"

"It isn't something to laugh at," said Anita. "It's a bad habit."

He looked suddenly very serious. "No, a wonderful one. If your Mother only did the same I would not be thinking now of going away again for good. But she doesn't. It's like the hair waving. You watch and see; she will forget about it and say the same thing tomorrow if she has to meet some man or other at the tea rooms. She can never tell the truth! She distorts everything so subtly that at first it was impossible for me to realize it. Her face — you can't imagine what an impression it made on me when I first saw it. She told you I am a painter? Well, I had not been able to paint for a year before I met her. After I met her the mere thought of her eyes, their shape, and that trembling of the nostrils, and the fine design of the mouth struck me like a fabulous discovery of what the mind could do to the flesh. It seemed almost transparently fine. I thought that just by coming near her I would see the beauty which moulded the exterior. It is so extraordinary, to have the power to give such a shock of beauty to others, to rouse them to do things. Wonderful things I painted from her, and then to find out . . ." He stopped abruptly. Then he saw in Anita's eyes such an imperious demand for truth, and he went on: "to find out that her eyes cover a continuous deception."

He got up tensely. "I don't suppose you relish the job of consoling me. It was wonderful of you to listen. But I think I'll be off again.

"No, don't go," said Anita, "I will talk to Mother."

Coming back from her rehearsal Anita found Vivien resting before dressing for the evening performance. She was lying down in the glamour of a coral night lamp. Anita sat on a low stool and admired her. Her face glowed with animation, and she was smiling at the remembrance of some pleasure.

Then Anita remembered her errand.

"I met Norman," she said.

"Oh, he's arrived! Is he in his room?" She rose as if to go to him.

"Wait," said Anita. "Let me tell you what I think of him. Doesn't it interest you?"

"Say so quickly," said Vivien.

"If he loved *me*," said Anita, "I think I would find it easy to love him alone."

"Oh, you think so," said Vivien laughing. "But I can't help myself — and anyway, I always come back to him."

"Don't you think he suffers?"

"Oh, no. I am careful."

"Why do you always submit?"

"I would despise myself if any formulas or ideas could control me. Being helpless before such impulses is simply a sign of being a real woman."

"You never talk about resistance!"

"Resistance is an arid thing, darling. Nothing grows of it but bitterness. It implies hardness; it dries up a woman physically and mentally."

"But his love, I should say, would be sufficient."

"Passion is exacting, my little Anita. It never thrives on an idea, an idea of faithfulness, for instance. It just demands whatever can inspire it. I have lived for it. I have never lost myself or been bored. I have loved white heat living. And the men who have a genius for white heat living are the very men who don't know how to make it last. Their own enthusiasms flare and die; and how blank the moments in between! They are dull, they are sleepy. One is forced to change."

"And in between, as you say," repeated Anita bitterly, "could you not find white heat living in your acting?"

"Oh, that," said Vivien, "means nothing to me."

Anita felt that for the moment there was nothing more she could say. Her Mother rose to begin her dressing. She turned on the lights in the lavender and silver bathroom. She examined her face in the mirror. "I am looking a little tired tonight," she said. Anita looked at Vivien's face in the mirror and was surprised to feel that it was no longer as beautiful as she had thought it the first day. The small incisive smile seemed oddly cold, and the slanting eyes calculating.

"I must go and get ready too," said Anita, and went away without the usual parting kiss.

Anita confessed her disappointment to Norman. He told her he had not expected anything from the talk, but he would wait. Perhaps Anita's own presence in the house might unconsciously change her Mother's attitude.

"Meanwhile," he said, "there is one thing which does me good, and that is work. I wish you would pose for me next week, in one of your costumes. I would like the purple train dress, and that typically gypsy gesture you make towards the end of the dance — like this — do you think you could hold such a pose? I work quickly. I won't tire you. I have an idea I could make something brilliant of it, with a footlight throwing shadows on your face. Will you do it? Come to my studio. Will the morning suit you? Say, an hour before lunch?"

There was such tenseness in his voice that Anita accepted and postponed many other things she had to do. When she arrived the first morning with her costume Norman had already prepared the canvas and was cleaning his palette. He seemed younger and relieved of his worries. He was eager over the pose, arranging the long ruffled train in a circle about her feet, interested in the odd bracelets, in the purple heels, in the intricately pinned flowers, in the tall purple comb. He changed and arranged a suitable background studying the effects of lights on her face. On the very model stand she tried two or three steps of the dance to obtain the pose, and when she came to the exact movement he called out to her and she stood still. He began the drawing in swift bold strokes, and talked to keep her interested. She watched him work.

The hour seemed very short to both of them. When Anita came down from the model's stand they realized they had forgotten Vivien in their talk.

Anita posed all that week, and also talked intimately with her Mother. The more they talked the more they realized the contrast between their ideas and feelings. Finally Vivien said: "Dear Anita, let's not talk anymore about Norman. It will change nothing. Let us just be friends — shall we? Someday when you yourself will be attracted to passion you will understand me better, someday when you really begin to live."

Anita the next morning went to Norman's studio with an altered face. He noticed it immediately. She did not hurry into the dressing room but lingered in front of the half finished painting.

"It's no use, Norman, Mother will never change. I have talked for hours with her. She thinks I am not fitted to advise her. And in a way, she is right. I am sorry." She did not dare look at his face. It seemed to her that she was taking Norman's unhappiness far too seriously, and she was beginning to wonder why she could not think of anything else.

He looked at her intently: "Don't worry, don't worry," he said, "it does not really matter anymore."

"Oh, you won't leave her," said Anita.

"I say it does not matter, Anita, because I don't love her anymore . . . I love *you*."

Anita stepped away from his open arms: "You love me because I look like her!"

"No, no," he cried out, "I love you, for your own sake, you who are an altogether different woman, Anita."

She saw in his eyes that he spoke the truth.

A strong curiosity, a secret desire for comparison drove Anita to talk to her Mother about it, without mentioning Norman's name. She needed to know her Mother's feelings, to know at once and in what way they were alike or different.

She spoke to her, her head timidly hidden against her so that she would not see her face; she blurted out talk of passion, of impulse, of a world-rocking desire. Vivien caressed her as if she had won back her real child, at last, as if at last there were a bond between them. She approved all her feelings, her surrender.

"But our love, our marriage will hurt another woman," said Anita. "What would you do in such a case?"

"*Don't think* of the other woman. *Nothing* must stand in the way of love, dear. You have been so foolish, so inflexible, so severe! I am so happy to see you soft and won, and beaten! Confess you are doubly happy, incredibly happy. Forget the other woman, foolish child. Go and enjoy your happiness."

And as Anita lifted her face, Vivien added: "Just that kiss has made you lovelier! Promise me you are not going to spoil it all with scruples."

Anita hid her face again.

All night she dwelt on how much she loved Norman, and why, and added with painstaking clarity all that he possessed that she loved in him: the smile which pitied as it smiled, the splendid shrewd face, the voice which surrounded her with a deep resonance, and lasted long after he spoke, his big presence, generous and powerful, his frankness, his talent. Feeling for him, for his life, the desire to make him altogether happy as she knew she could seemed to sweep all else before it, and yet, stronger than the need of him and the love of him was another feeling.

All that Vivien had said counted little because it did not include love such as she understood it. But Anita wanted to have the courage to do what her Mother had never done: resist. Resist for the sake of denying herself a happiness which hurt another, resist for the sake of testing herself, of measuring the depths between her character and Vivien's. Vivien's life and ways and selfishness revolted her. But how could she sacrifice Norman to such a test, to her obsession with an ideal? She had loved ideals so! While Vivien had sought tests of her physical power Anita had sought many times the exultant feeling of mastering herself, of plying herself to a difficult ideal, such as her Mother despised.

She did not keep her thoughts from Norman, but they did not surprise him. "I love you for that," he told her.

"If I follow her own urgings," said Anita, "then our love and marriage should come before all else, the fulfillment of it before all scruples. Vivien said nothing should stand in the way of one's desires."

"She has told you that? Then you can do it?"

"*Because* she has told me that I can't do it. Whatever she would do, Norman, is just what I don't want to do."

"But Anita, our love . . ."

"I don't want our love to resemble hers, Norman, our life to be like hers. She said, when I talked to her, that she was glad my own resistance was broken at last because now I would understand and approve her life."

"It doesn't matter what she said, Anita. We know our love is something else, something she cannot understand."

"I would like to do the thing she has never done: resist."

"But you would not sacrifice me to such a test!"

He was holding her. He felt her love and her struggle, and her indecision.

"I love you for that courage, Anita, but don't ruin our love. I love you to be strong, but not inflexible!" He teased her, he kissed and begged. That evening he called for her after the show and was very tender, and Anita felt half conquered, half won.

But the next day she was gone from the house. Norman knew what her going away meant. In desperation he went to Vivien. She noticed the alteration of his face.

"So it's you she loved!" she exclaimed. "And how could *you* love such a woman! She lives only for her own foolish ideas!"

"You can't understand her," he said sadly.

"Oh, yes I can. She was not human, that's all. I myself could never be so hard and cruel. She has hurt you and me. I have never done things like that. She would have made you more unhappy than I ever did. After all, I am soft, am I not?"

Norman was so used to her acting, he did not look at her face. He sat next to her, dejectedly.

"You both said you loved me."

"Yes, but in such different ways! I because I am too human, Anita because she is not human! I think you ought to love me better, Norman." Vivien came close to him, very gently, and stroked his face. "How she has made you suffer! Stay with me. I will make you forget it." She surrounded him with a new solicitude. "It would be so much wiser. Don't try to find her."

But he stood up brusquely, looking into her eyes: "Goodbye. You are not so very different. You have both hurt me but I prefer to be made unhappy by Anita's way rather than by yours." Then, reaching for his hat and coat: "I am not going to stop until I find her."